EROS

Eros

BEYOND THE DEATH DRIVE

Rosaura Martínez Ruiz

TRANSLATED BY RAMSEY McGLAZER

FOREWORD BY JUDITH BUTLER

FORDHAM UNIVERSITY PRESS   NEW YORK 2021

Fordham University Press gratefully acknowledges financial assistance and support provided for the publication of this book by the Facultad de Filosofía y Letras of the Universidad Nacional Autónoma de México.

This book was originally published in Spanish as Rosaura Martínez Ruiz, *Eros: Más allá de la pulsión de muerte*, published by Siglo XXI Editores, 2018.

Fordham University Press also publishes its books in a variety of electronic formats. Some content that appears in print may not be available in electronic books.

Visit us online at www.fordhampress.com.

Library of Congress Cataloging-in-Publication Data available online at https://catalog.loc.gov.

Printed in the United States of America

23 22 21 5 4 3 2 1

First edition

Contents

Foreword

Judith Butler

As a philosopher, Rosaura Martínez Ruiz reads Freud and Derrida to offer a creative and compelling formulation of key debates within psychoanalysis, including the relation between pleasure and destruction, memory and transformation, and the role of negation in public and political life. Through a rereading of Freud's *Project for a Scientific Psychology* (1895), she opens up the field of lived memory as a site of alteration, modification, and unexpected openings for the future. Throughout, Martínez makes clear how psychoanalysis can open up an ethical and erotic pathway for a conflictual public sphere. At the same time, she argues that Freud gives us a way to think beyond destruction if only we probe the potentials of Eros.

The investigations into memory in this text allow Martínez to open up a reflection on life that accepts negation, but opposes destruction. At first, this argument might seem paradoxical, but for Martínez this Freudian way of thinking preexists both the discovery of the pleasure principle as the primary structure of psychic life in *The Interpre-*

tation of Dreams (1905) and the later turn to the death drive in *Beyond the Pleasure Principle* (1920), which has formed the basis of a dualistic understanding of the psyche. Understanding Freud's account in 1895 of how memories can be transformed or modified and the psychic trajectories to which they give rise offers a perspective on what can happen within the clinical setting and, more generally, public forms of trauma. For Martínez, life itself is characterized both by the desire for excitation and the conservative longing for stasis and preservation, and this oscillation should be understood as a permutation of Eros itself. In effect, Martínez takes on the burden of explaining why destructiveness is not a reason to posit a separate and rival death drive. In her view, Eros is not simply "binding" but holds within it the very disturbance allocated to the death drive. In the service of her argument, she points out (a) that the death drive never works without an erotic component and (b) that Eros is itself riddled with negativity: possibilities of breakage and fissure.

Thus, Martínez's book challenges two truisms related to psychoanalytic theory. The first is that Freud abandoned his early project to recover memories and seek catharsis in favor of a view that posits pleasure and wish-fulfillment as the primary tendency of psychic life. The second is that Freud gave up his views on the primacy of pleasure when he introduced the death drive as a rival psychic tendency. In accord with her reading of Freud's early reflections on memories and mnemic traces, she effectively argues that the abandoned stages of Freud's thought continue in the latter, persisting as they are subject to modification and contribute to new trajectories of his thought.

The argument above would have been enough for a monograph of this kind. But Martínez takes this argument a step further. Derrida's engagement with Freud gives us a way to understand how memory works. Indeed, memory works, in her view, as writing. Relying both on Derrida's call to find a way to live beyond "sovereign cruelty" and his considerations of the "mystic writing-pad" to establish his theory of the trace, Martínez suggests that deconstruction (of the Derridean kind) helps to illuminate the semiotic (or cultural, in her terms) and ethical potentials of psychoanalysis for our times.

Indeed, it is not only that Derrida illuminates underappreciated potentials in Freud, but that a philosophy of life that opposes strategies of annihilation (one way that Martínez defines fascism) would do well to build on the insights of both Freud and Derrida. Her title begins emphatically with "Eros" and then continues subversively with "beyond the death drive." In this way, she reverses Freud's own title, *Beyond the Pleasure Principle*, which implies that "the death drive" is the name for what is beyond. In his name, Martínez reverses Freud's title, a subversive form of loyalty. To go "beyond the death drive" requires that we return to the early Freud in order to unlearn the developmental history in which his corpus is generally taught and to remember what he taught us there. Indeed, her contentious wager is that Freud gives us in the *Project* the basic tools we need to refuse the later dualism between pleasure and the death drive. In this way, Martínez has entered the long and fractious debate on how to understand that dualism as a permutation of both life and Eros. Thus, she demonstrates to some degree what it means to enter into a conflictual field without the aim of annihilation (of oneself or another). Read as a continuous sentence, her title implies that Eros is beyond the death drive, thus reversing the historical periodization of Freud's discoveries by insisting that Freud should be read through his own model of temporality, one that affirms that the trace of the past repeats in the present in altered form.

Martínez is mindful that she has to account for those features of psychic life which have come to be named by the death drive. In her view, pleasure is primary, and the death drive is a permutation of the pleasure principle, found in the "erotic fractures" it produces. What is "beyond" the pleasure principle is, in her view, not a fully independent second principle (only pleasure is a *Prinzip*, not death). What is called the death drive is better understood through a Derridean conception of the limit against which the pleasure principle intermittently founders, especially when pleasure takes aggressive and cruel forms, or when pleasure is reduced at the hands of cruelty. On the one hand, the "limit" opens up to the field of alterity: other people, obtrusive worlds, surfaces and fabrics of the social. On the other hand, this limit is part of the life of pleasure and even proves to be the condition of possibility for action. "Externality" is the name for all that makes a seamless pursuit of gratification difficult. What is "foreign" is not necessarily inhabiting a world that is external to the ego. Indeed, the very distinction between interior and exterior emerges as a consequence of what she calls the limit. And it is in light of the limit that that differentiating mechanism that generates that distinction can be rightly understood. We know the claim often made in the context of child psychology that early expressions of aggression and expulsion are necessary to secure a boundaried sense of self. A child pushes the parent away, and we think, "oh good, the child is differentiating," by which we mean, "emerging as separate." For Martínez, the argument is more general and philosophical. The limit that belongs to the life of pleasure, without which pleasure cannot be thought, is the better name for the death drive, one that does not invite speculation on its drive status or topographic location in the mind. If her thesis is right, then she has found a new way to link psychoanalysis and deconstruction in the course of developing an ethics and politics that not only refuses to annihilate alterity but cultivates erotic practices for that purpose.

One of the driving political arguments of this text is that we live in a world in which the encounter with difference too often culminates in denunciation, repression, exclusion, or annihilation. One could conclude that her view is that the sovereign cruelty of the world can, and should, be overcome through recognizing Eros as the truer and better sovereign. But that misses the point that Eros contains within it the potential to dismantle sovereignty in favor of a different sense of sociality, one that prizes heterogeneity without seeking recourse to a unifying principle or the goal of harmony.

How, then, is this field of differences opened, and what potentials does it carry? Martínez reminds her reader that Derridean deconstruction, broadly understood, is a critique of metaphysical presence. The term *diffférance* is spoken the same way as difference in French, suggesting that the differences between signs cannot be registered through recourse to voice. The human voice, as it were, falls away with the new graphic formation. And the term then indicates the displacement of both human origin and human presence. Whatever mark becomes a trace of this kind functions as an oscillation between presence and absence. When the mark does not carry or manifest the presence of the author, redemptive and reparative fantasies are undermined. The graphic cannot yield the human, at least not exactly. It yields, in fact, the dilemma of not being able to return to the human behind the writing. That dashed expectation is one that structures psychoanalytic thinking as well. A work of mourning has already begun with every act of writing, separated as it is from voice, and the expectation that voice delivers or manifests a human presence. In her view, writing does register that someone was present at some time, but that that moment of coincidence quickly disappears when the trace remains, and the writer does not. If we seek to bring back that presence, we fail; it is only through memory that some sort of re-presentation is possible, but that is neither a return nor a recovery.

This key point, that it is only through memory's re-presentation that some indirect access to what is lost becomes possible, becomes crucial to the book's argument. It is also the point at which Derrida meets Freud. In "A Note Upon the 'Mystic Writing-Pad'" (1925), Freud comments upon the way that writing on the pad disappears when the page is lifted from the pad, but then, once vanished, the writing leaves its impression on the pad that overlaps with myriad other such impressions. Some marks crowd out others, but others are changed by virtue of encroachment, proximity, overlapping space. In the end, however, mnemic traces merge so that it is not always possible to know which are prior, and which are later. Martínez writes: "[M]emory is like a tissue of overlapping mnemic traces, and it involves a historicity in which time is a conflictual and not harmonious phenomenon." To say that the mystic pad, like memory, bears different temporal modalities does not mean that they are organized or synthesized by the pad. Memory does not synthesize in that way. Those temporalities appear only in fragmented form, occasionally fusing with one another and producing new effects. To the degree that this process is unconscious and, as Freud insists, the unconscious knows no negation, such traces never go away. And yet they are perpetually subject to alteration, linked with other memories, worked over by other temporalities. For Martínez, the mnemic trace establishes that connection between memory and writing as well as the fact that the trace is subject to modifications to come, including "working through" and the opening of new horizons of futurity.

How do we understand the relation of this potentially and perpetually modified mnemic trace to the future? Memory persists by virtue of a certain intensity, and this can be understood as the force with which inscription takes place on a page (or pad). The writing instrument requires pressure, and the writing surface always resists this inscription. Indeed, without that resistance, the obduracy of that external surface to inscription, writing itself could not take place. Writing requires resistance to make its mark. For Martínez, writing is a mnemic trace requiring resistance, and "writing" becomes a way to understand psychic process, particularly memory. She shows how this works by examining the description of neuronal activity in the *Project*, treating that "neurological fiction" as a heuristic for understanding memory and the new effects it brings into being. Memory, now understood as mnemic traces accumulating and altering associations and effects through time, does not return us to the past, but can, within psychoanalysis, lead us to different future trajectories. But this can only happen if memories are not subject to repression, exclusion, or attempted annihilation. This brings us back to the question of how memories are pushed out or repressed through the construction of psychic borders as violent as they are fragile. The rejection of a wish considered taboo takes place not just through a single act, but through a defensive construction that has clear state and military associations. That wish is outside of me, not mine, exists, if it does, over there, in the external world. Indeed, the strict distinction between internal and external worlds is an effect of this kind of exclusionary psychic operation.

Martínez is clear: Fascism is the violence of total exclusion. She offers a critical rejoinder to its lure: "Proactive resistance" can counter destructive tendencies understood as the radical exclusion of what is considered "foreign" no matter whether that is a foreignness in the ego or in the world, or a confused representation and fusion of the two. Martínez asks what happens when the psyche wards off what arrives from an organism that is other or, at least, experienced as alien. How is that differentiated field of life suppressed or refused? And can we understand that expulsion precisely as a refusal to be changed and modified by a new encounter with alterity? When the psyche seeks to expel precisely what promises to alter it, it loses a chance, the chance to acknowledge, and be changed by, the differentiated structure of the living world. One's sense of the nation and the world can and does change when one concedes to the demand to be changed by what is new. The future that opens is one that openly avows the possibility of giving space to difference, opposing forms of expulsion whose ultimate form is annihilation. The opposition to annihilation as politics or, rather, as the end to the political field, requires an openness to being touched and altered by the encounter with difference, but also to a process of public life that is not fully calculable.

There are plenty of resistances to being changed by what is other, considered foreign, especially if it means revising fundamental notions of religious, national, racial, and territorial belonging. And yet to be open to the future is precisely an openness to being changed by what one encounters, a struggle with and against those forms of resistance that would seal the boundaries of selfhood. One reason Martínez then argues for freedom of expression within the public sphere, one that includes polemical encounters and confrontations, is that it allows for this struggle with alterity in open fora. To explain this process, she introduces the idea of the "*duelo*," understood complexly as a duet, a form of battle and a form of mourning. To lose someone or, indeed, an ideal of the nation is to be transformed by loss, and to carry the trace of what is lost. There is no way to mourn without mourning being altered by the other, which is why Freud describes the ego as the precipitate of a history of loss, a geological formation in which the myriad traces of loss are sedimented (*The Ego and the Id*, 1923). The "*duelo*" contains within it the losses to be mourned, the changes demanded by the new world born of loss, the world in which what is lost is no longer there, and the resistance to that acknowledgment and that transformation. In this way, the "*duelo*" for Martínez is a "political practice that is also erotic."

Lastly, the erotic itself is reconfigured by this text, found in the mnemic trace or rather the "mnemic trace archive" that carries both loss and life. Martínez's explanation gives us a way to understand the title in a new light. There is no beyond the pleasure principle, in her view, because what we call the "death drive" is the conservative and regressive tendency that subtends, and punctuates, all Eros. I am not sure I can agree with this argument, since the forms of traumatic unpleasure and their relentless repetitions denoted by the death drive seem not to be contained or explained by the economies of pleasure. Freud remarked that the death drive can be discerned in the circuitous route to death that characterizes the life trajectory of the organism in *Beyond the Pleasure Principle*. Although many have read this as the workings of the death drive in forms of self-sabotage, for instance, Martínez considers that the clustering of mnemic traces functions in the service of life, seeking to delay death without denying its inevitability. The instances of "negation" usually understood as exemplifying the death drive are here reconfigured to show that the death drive can be bent in the service of life. Sublimation is one such example Martínez offers, deriving her analysis in part from Paul Ricoeur. Humor is another to the extent that it finds its way around the death-dealing force of the superego. There is a general claim here, again philosophical, that reveals the singularity and the life-affirmation at the heart of this project:

> Negation is, in this same sense, a detour or rerouting of the destructive drive, not a renunciation of it. Playing and art follow this same path. When Freud says that the study of judgment is the royal road to an understanding of negation and thinks of the latter as a path taken by the death drive, he is referring to the realm of language. There is thus a basis in Freud for the effort to connect the psyche to language defined as a semiotic function, since negation is implicated in language at every turn. Negation speaks through the patient who says, "No, she's not my mother," and the psychoanalyst knows that she is the patient's mother but displaced by a representation, that is, symbolized by another object that allows for fantasy, for dreaming, or for acting "as if the real were not." In the same way, art and play are also the irruptions of a negativity that cannot be reduced to destructiveness. In the symbolic, the death drive reveals its capacity not for pure destruction, but rather, on the contrary, for enjoyable creation, because it manages to overcome absence, passivity, loss, and the mediated satisfaction of desire in general.

This new book challenges us to rethink who we are, to what world we belong, and how best to engage the challenge to change and create in a world in which state powers continue to exercise forms of cruelty in the name of exclusion and destruction. Martínez asks us to consider what it means to be members of an erotic battalion, those who seek and enact love in public space to defeat the forces of destruction that so often cover their traces. This theory asks us to practice proactive resistance as a collectivity, to take up negation, erotically and ethically, to dismantle sovereign cruelty and to oppose, in all its forms, annihilation.

March 15, 2021

EROS

Introduction

On July 10, 2000, Jacques Derrida gave a lecture in Paris at a meeting of psychoanalysts organized by Élisabeth Roudinesco, a historian of psychoanalysis, and by the analyst René Major. The call to participate in this meeting was interesting and unprecedented in that it was open. Challenging the tendency of psychoanalytic communities to organize only endogenous gatherings, Roudinesco and Major decided to plan a gathering "without surnames," that is, an exchange among psychoanalysts rather than among Freudians, Kleinians, or Lacanians, and so on. Because of its scale and especially its aims, the organizers named the conference the States General of Psychoanalysis, echoing the name of the French assembly that was a precursor of the Revolution and that gathered together the representatives of all powers. Derrida's lecture, titled "Psychoanalysis Searches the States of Its Soul," also had a subtitle that is very suggestive and, from my perspective, challenging as well: "The Impossible Beyond of a Sovereign Cruelty." More than a lecture, Derrida's intervention was a call, a complaint, and a solicitation addressed to the whole psychoanalytic community, one that sought to reckon with the problem of violence. Derrida's reproach had to do with the dearth or even the outright lack of psychoanalytic participation in the political realm. For Derrida, after the Freudian discovery of the death drive, defined as a tendency toward destruction inherent in human nature, one cannot say anything about violence or especially about cruelty without recourse to psychoanalysis. Although of course psychoanalysis on its own is not sufficient for thinking through these problems, nothing can be said about them without psychoanalysis. It is true, Derrida adds, that the world has resisted and still resists psychoanalysis. But psychoanalysts, too, have resisted and still resist the world when they have not reflected, and do not reflect upon, the problem of cruelty, defined as making suffer or causing pain merely for the sake of pleasure. (Here Derrida mentions all of the meanings that Freud discovers in causing suffering, which can also be a reflexive act: making suffer, letting suffer, making oneself suffer, letting oneself make suffer, and so on.) Derrida is right: With notable exceptions, the psychoanalytic community has been irresponsible and conservative. I would therefore like to offer this text as a response to Derrida's invitation, as a commentary on his text "Psychoanalysis Searches the States of Its Soul: The Impossible Beyond of a Sovereign Cruelty." The pages that follow not only constitute a text; they also form a letter and deliver a call, an interpellation. What follows is my response in the form of a series of reflections not on cruelty—I have not undertaken to write a treatise on this concept—but rather on the "beyond" in Derrida's subtitle.

The "beyond" in the title of Sigmund Freud's *Beyond the Pleasure Principle* promises that that text will discuss a psychic tendency that is not subject to the pleasure principle. But this promise remains unfulfilled: In fact there is nothing, for Freud, beyond the pleasure principle, which is sovereign. Nevertheless, in this same text, Freud locates certain forces before or on "this side" of the pleasure principle's "dominance" (SE 18: 9),[1] and others that somehow emerge in order to modify the pleasure principle, that is, in order to alter its rhythm and its cadence, at least temporarily. It would thus seem that the text makes clear that the pleasure principle is an insuperable limit, but although Derrida does not engage in an in-depth elucidation, he does gesture toward possible detours around this kind of uncrossable boundary or limit, or the pleasure principle when it takes the form of the death drive, aggressivity, or cruelty. This book deals with these fissures in the sovereignty of the pleasure principle, which I will call erotic fractures.

This calls for an analysis of the idea of an ethical imperative that moves action beyond two sets of limits. I am referring to both the limits that an unstable, contingent, and circumstantial reality—the kind of reality that contemporary ontologies describe—places on the human capacity for ethical and political calculation, and the limits that the death drive places on projects for peaceful coexistence and the love of otherness. I will thus need to explore and elucidate the notion of a need to pass beyond the beyond, clarifying what is meant by the oxymoronic claim that the limit is a site of possibility in ontological, political, and ethical terms. More than a limit, the ontology of separation is the condition of possibility for truly revolutionary, and not just what we could call reformist, action.

What remains after these reflections is the task of building, on the basis of a deconstructive reading, a strong argument for responsible social action among social subjects. This argument is based on two central ideas: First, that although, in ontological terms, being has no immutable foundation—and this could be interpreted as a lack that renders both decision-making and right action impossible — "unfounded" being in fact opens the possibility of a transformation in all semiotic relations. Culture, defined as a text or linguistic fabric, is open to being rewritten, and in this sense the subject is a sign that can be grafted actively into the text and can alter it. Responsible action is thus both revolutionary and desirable. Second, we must ask whether, in general, remaining vigilant against, denouncing, and resisting all forms of discrimination, exclusion, and annihilation of difference should be privileged as the swords and shields protecting us from what is arguably insuperable: a natural tendency toward violence against what is different.

What I hope to make clear by the end of this text is that deconstruction is a privileged place from which to glimpse the horizon where the limit becomes a site of possibility. What is deconstruction? In the first instance, it is a way of inhabiting thought (Cragnolini, "Derrida") and the world that brings together at least three key philosophical fields: ontology, semiotics, and politics. Deconstruction is, on the one hand, a critical operation that targets all semiotic phenomena whose damaging consequences involve the exclusion or annihilation of otherness. On the other hand, deconstruction opens onto an ontology in which being is not pure or full presence. This ontology lets us recognize "what is [*lo que está*]," "what presents itself," as shot through with "what is *not* [*lo que no está*]" in several senses: with what is no longer, with what is not yet, with what never was, and with what will not be. To redeploy Derrida's metaphor, being turns out to be haunted by specters, where "haunting" is a form of being [*estar*] in a place without fully occupying it. In this way, ghosts or specters inhabit what is [*lo que es*], not by conquering it, but by being there, announcing themselves without presenting themselves, not showing themselves, but doing things, producing effects. They are like the ghosts that are not present in a room and yet move objects and make noises within it.

Deconstruction is also a strategy, a means by which to approach the horizon of two tasks: first, the dismantling of semiotic relations to reveal that there is no strong ontological foundation that sustains them, and, second, the denunciation of the effects of (or the meanings associated with) the repression, exclusion, and even annihilation of what is different from the dominant. This is why Derrida calls ontology *hauntology*:[2] because being does not have an ultimate, immutable foundation, whether in the form of logos, substance, reason, nature, or God. In hauntology, being oscillates or plays between presence and absence. It is an "apparition" that we know does not belong to the present; what we do not know is whether it comes from the past or the future. What is [*lo que es*] is the difference between what has been and what has not yet been, what has not been and what will not be. And a difference is not a full presence; for this reason, we can no longer speak in terms of substance, unless we revise our understanding of that term.

But beyond being a critique of the metaphysics of presence (which thinks of being as consummated and determined in and as the present of its appearance) and a critique of culture, and in addition to developing a *sui generis* ontology, deconstruction is also itself a political act, a strategic intervention that seeks to transform all systems of signification, with culture being the greatest and most powerful of these. As Umberto Eco writes, "[T]he whole of culture *should* be studied as a communicative phenomenon based on signification systems" (*A Theory of Semiotics* 22; emphasis in original). This means not only that culture can be studied in this way, but that it is only by studying culture in this way that its basic mechanisms can be clarified. Deconstruction's privileged strategy is the unveiling of what is behind signs;

this is a form of semiotics, because the latter is "*the discipline studying everything which can be used in order to lie*" (Eco, *A Theory of Semiotics* 7; emphasis in original).

But let us continue to think of deconstruction as a critical operation that takes on the metaphysics of presence. Since the twentieth century, the philosophical quest for the essence, origin, and ultimate foundation of all that is has been seen as complicit with totalitarian discourses, forms of racial persecution, general discrimination, the mistreatment of animals, and the human exploitation of natural resources (where to name these as "resources" is already an exercise of domination). In other words, philosophical discourse and the metaphysical effort to locate being on a foundation that we could think of as unitary, as One, have been interpreted by contemporary ontologies as part of the political machinery that represses difference. Put differently, the philosophical gesture of distinguishing between substance and accident is one that excludes, represses, denies, and even annihilates difference, the accidental, the weak, and so on. Nevertheless, like psychic repression, this exclusion of difference produces symptoms; that is, it gives rise to effects in speech, language, and culture in general. For Derrida, the history of philosophy is the history of efforts to repress all that is not identical with what, in a given context, is thought of as strong, reasonable, conscious, phallic, white, and so on.

Following Nietzsche and Heidegger, among others, Derrida argues that this ontology has no phenomenological foundation. What actually appears is a tension between what is present and what is not, between what is and what is not. An entity's being is also defined by what it is not, what it was not, what it is not yet, and what it will not be. This, among other things, is what Derrida means when he suggests that *différance* is—or is at—the origin.

The Derridean neographism *diffférance* (from the French

différence, with an e) seeks to shed light on several problems in the history of thought. It is a word that embodies all of the preoccupations of deconstruction. And beyond being a word, this orthographic act of violence is a simulacrum, a performative that discloses or unveils. It shows ontology to be hauntology and refutes the claim that speech predominates over writing, a claim that in semiotics, as in all philosophy, had been interpreted as a guardian and messenger of truth, since the voice was thought to be a presence, and presence was thought to be a condition of possibility for truth. Finally, *différance* also demonstrates how a linguistic act can transform the history of thought.

First, *différance* (with an a) seeks to recover the sense of spatiality and temporality recessed in *différence* (with an e).[3] *Différer* is a verb that can be used to indicate the difference between entities that are discernibly non-identical, but it can also designate a temporal or spatial deferral or delay, as when one postpones something for later. Although *différence* does not immediately evoke this second meaning, Derrida's orthographic shift is a way of calling attention to the temporalization and spatialization that are necessarily at play in any differential relation. In French, however, *différence* and *différance* are pronounced in the same way; there is no phonetic difference, so that the only way a listener can know whether one or the other word is being used is to refer to the written word. This necessity is key for Derrida, since it shows that it is false to argue that the voice, defined as presence, is privileged in truthful communication. Finally, *différance* is ontologically the origin of everything that is:

> What is written as *différance*, then, will be the playing movement that "produces"—by means of something that is not simply an activity—these differences, these effects of difference. This does not mean

> that the *différance* that produces differences is somehow before them, in a simple and unmodified—in-different—present. *Différance* is the non-full, non-simple, structured, and differentiating origin of differences. Thus, the name "origin" no longer suits it. ("Différance," in *Margins of Philosophy* 11)

What presents itself, what appears, is an effect of differences of force, instinct, quantity, possibility, and so on. But if we are dealing with differences, then we can no longer speak of presences, of pure and fully present substances. This is why Derrida crosses out all of these giant words in the philosophical vocabulary. ~~Presence~~ signals that being is what appears and at the same time what does not appear. The strikethrough is retained in order to let us see that we are dealing with an economy and not with total negativity. Absence determines being; lack accompanies being as a possibility; negativity, like what is not, is inherent to being. This is therefore an absence that "is" in the sense that it produces effects. This does not mean that what is not becomes present or presents itself. Still, it announces itself. What ~~presents~~ itself does so in the form of a trace, a mark, something undecidable that at once announces a presence and declares an absence.[4] What is a trace—what is writing—if not the witness or testament to the absence of a presence, or to the presence of an absence?

It is in this sense that Derrida argues that the economy of being is the economy of writing. And the latter is the effect of an encounter, or a difference made by the collision, of two or more forces of distinct quantities, where some are more powerful than others. The result of this encounter is the inscription that the greater quantity leaves on the weaker one. We should not lose sight of the fact that the latter must be a quantity capable of offering resistance, because it is the difference between resistance and violence that gives rise to writing; that is, if the force of the weaker quantity is not sufficient for resistance, then the effect will not be writing but rather conquest and annihilation, in which the stronger force will take the place of the weaker one. In short, in order for there to be writing, there must be a force that resists.

Writing not only involves an economy of space; it also involves a singular temporality. The trace or mark, like the specter, announces a past presence and a possible future re-presentation in the form of a memory. This, then, is an economy that involves a temporality that is neither linear nor harmonious. It is an implosive temporality (Martínez Ruiz, "Alterability" 531).

In "Freud and the Scene of Writing," Derrida draws on the analogy in which Freud compares the psyche to a written artifact, describing the process by which a trace is formed as a temporal phenomenon. There is a time of writing; the inscription of the trace depends on an economy of discontinuity, that is, on a space between the exertion of pressure and its interruption. A continuity of stimulation has neither quality nor meaning.

In "A Note Upon the 'Mystic Writing-Pad,'" Freud describes the same phenomenon in connection with the time of the psyche. In this curious text, memory is represented by a small wax tablet in a writing mechanism made up of three layers. Freud is referring to a children's toy, a "mystic writing pad" [*pizarra mágica*, or, in German, *Wunderblock*] that is mystic, magical, or marvelous (*wunderbar*) precisely because it fulfills two functions that no implement for writing (say, chalkboard or sheet of paper) can fulfill simultaneously: It allows for the unlimited reception of signs and makes it possible to store these signs in perpetuity. The particular design of this artifact allows one to save what one writes even while one writes it; and if one erases what one has written, this erasure is only apparent, because a part of the pad saves everything that is inscribed on it. Both of these two functions can be fulfilled because the pad is a layered mechanism. I have already noted that it has three layers. The last of these is a slab of dark wax placed on a board; above this is a waxed, transparent sheet and another, made of celluloid, that serves to protect the middle layer so that it is not torn. These two sheets are attached to the mechanism at the top and left unattached at the bottom. The most interesting thing about the pad is that no ink is necessary in order to write on its surface; this is instead done with a needle that records the inscriptions on the wax layer. When it's drawn on, the waxed-paper layer sticks to the wax layer, and the impression becomes perceptible. But if this contact is broken, the writing disappears. In this way, the mechanism's capacity for reception is unlimited. But so too is its capacity for storage, for archiving, because, as Freud describes it, the disappearance or erasure of what's written here is only an illusion. If we lift the celluloid sheet and the waxed paper, we can see all of the traces that have been left on the wax slab beneath.

The time that Freud identifies as the effect of the interruption of excitation—or of writing, in the case of the mystic writing pad—can be thought of as the time of the metaphysics of presence. This temporality that is continuous and fluid, and that can be thought of as an accumulation and sequence of presents, is not the temporality of the unconscious. The temporality of the unconscious is an economy of overwriting. Memory is like a tissue of overlapping mnemic traces, and it involves a historicity in which time is a conflictual and not a harmonious phenomenon.[5]

The time of memory defined as writing—that is, as text—is implosive. The Spanish Royal Academy's *Dictionary of the*

Spanish Language notes that implosion is the "act of breaking inward, in a collapse of the walls of a cavity when these walls exert less pressure than an external force." In a written text, the past, present, and future are fragmented, although these times do not disperse, but are brought together.[6] This is not an *ex*plosion because the past, present, and future are not burst apart; they are not separated and do not veer off in different directions, because the direction of the breakage is inward. They are mixed and even, in some cases, fused. Here the past, present, and future overlap and are confused with one another, making it impossible to differentiate with total precision between the events of the past and those of the present as well as the future. This temporality is not exclusive to psychic writing; it is the temporality of all writing, and for Derrida being is writing.

Another theoretically consequential problem that Freud points to in this text but that has not been closely studied either by Freud or by Derrida is that mnemic traces are "permanent—even though *not unalterable*" (SE 19: 228; my emphasis). In the model of the mystic writing pad, the wax slab has a perimeter and a delimited surface, so that every trace that is inscribed on it will fill its area, writing over what has already been drawn. And what has already been inscribed will make the new marks follow certain paths; that is, it will shape the new traces. Writing on the mystic writing pad, like writing in the psyche, is overwriting.

For this reason, the future plays a key role, because the mnemic trace is always open to modifications to come. This openness is performative in the sense that it alters or modifies the mnemic trace at every moment. Memory, like human existence, although it is historical, "gazes" toward the future. What is memory if not a recollection to come?

Freud's text on the mystic writing pad concludes this way:

> If we imagine one hand writing upon the surface of the Mystic Writing-Pad while another periodically raises its covering-sheet from the wax slab, we shall have a concrete representation of the way in which I tried to picture the functioning of the perceptual apparatus of our mind. (SE 19: 232)

There is writing and erasure, that is, archiving and forgetting. What matters at this point is that both happen at the same time. It is not that the trace is first drawn and later erased; it is instead a matter of the instant, of the imperceptible moment in which the impression and the wax are confused. In other words, what opens a space for new writing is the fact that earlier writing is erased. But this loss is in fact a fusion: The sign absorbs its context and at the same time resignifies it. This resignification is not only a matter of a sign with different meanings that depend on the place into which it is inserted; this modification of meaning originates in a double scene where, on the one hand, context changes, but, on the other, the sign itself is modified. Rewriting has this twofold effect: The context modifies the sign—we could even think in terms of the modification of its architecture—but this context is also altered *by* the sign. The double scene and double effect call for a temporal spacing. The hand that writes must take breaks and suspend the pressure it applies in order to leave traces and not, say, holes, because writing is a matter of a delicate and fragile difference, where the force that intrudes must not annihilate and the one that receives must not close off, exclude, or cancel out the one that bursts in.[7] There must be a movement that opens space and time. According to Derrida:

> Temporality as spacing will be not only the horizontal discontinuity of a chain of signs, but also will be writing as the interruption and restoration of contact

> between the various depths of psychical levels: the remarkably heterogeneous temporal fabric of psychical work itself. We find neither the continuity of a line nor the homogeneity of a volume; only the differentiated depth of a stage, and its spacing. ("Freud and the Scene of Writing," in *Writing and Difference* 225)

The implosive temporality of writing is, moreover, what makes ontology hauntology:

> Let us call [this] a *hauntology*. This logic of haunting would not be merely larger and more powerful than an ontology or than a thinking of Being (of the "to be," assuming that it is a matter of Being in the "to be or not to be," but nothing is less certain). It would harbor within itself, but like circumscribed places or particular effects, eschatology and teleology themselves. It would *comprehend* them, but incomprehensibly. How to *comprehend* in fact the discourse of the end or the discourse about the end? Can the extremity of the extreme ever be comprehended? And the opposition between "to be" and "not to be"? *Hamlet* already began with the expected return of the dead King. After the end of history, the spirit comes by *coming back* [*revenent*], it figures *both* a dead man who comes back and a ghost whose expected return repeats itself, again and again. (*Specters* 10)

But if the specter returns compulsively, then we need to ask whether we could ever experience something like "the end of history," since the return of the ghost is in keeping with the logic of iterability, that is, of repetition in difference. According to this logic, every event modifies both memory and destiny at the same time. The most interesting thing about this claim is that what being is and undergoes includes not just what it was and what it undergoes now or carries as an inheritance, but also what it will be and not be in the future. The very idea of the specter refers to this expectant projection; its ominousness derives from the fact that it can "appear"—or not—at any moment and under any circumstance. In this sense, history is in fact always to come, or has yet to be inscribed, and ontological experience is immersed in the logic of the a posteriori, constantly displaced and deferred. But this is a delay that is also always a matter of radical hope.

The now, Heidegger says, is nothing more than a "discoursing articulation of a *making present* that temporalizes itself in unity with an awaiting that retains" (*Being and Time* 382). When we say "now," we most often refer, without realizing it, to other times. We say "now," and we imply, "now that this has happened," or "now as soon as I've finished this, I'll do that." The now moves always toward the past and toward the future. There are no pure times. The present is not a pure "now"; the past has not yet been, and the future has already been. Any phenomenon will involve new dimensions as time passes, and this is not just because of its reinterpretation, but rather because there is change, that is, because the existence of things alters itself, as do memory traces, because new events gradually modify both history and the future. It is in this sense that history has yet to be written. But this "not yet" can and must be freeing and not paralyzing.

This contingency makes being phenomenologically open to alteration. And this openness or ontological fissuring make it impossible to think here of a foundation, origin, or essence. As Mónica Cragnolini explains:

> As a philosophy of thresholds, hauntology moves "between": between the living and the dead, between

> the past and hope for the future. But this "between" does not presuppose a space for any possible dialecticization, but rather a realm of uncertainty that cannot be sealed shut by any dialectic or by any synthesis. This "between" presupposes a disjunction of the present that complicates philosophies of presence and, along with them, all logics of identity centered on the same. ("Una ontología" 235–241)

Openness toward the future is therefore radical.

This phenomenology is related to an ontology in which the only thing that is radically erased is essence. Derrida writes:

> The trace is the erasure of selfhood, of one's own presence, and is constituted by the threat or anguish of its irremediable disappearance, of the disappearance of its disappearance. An unerasable trace is not a trace, it is a full presence, an immobile and uncorruptible substance, a son of God, a sign of parousia and not a seed, that is, a mortal germ. ("Freud and the Scene of Writing," in *Writing and Difference* 230)

This rift, this being fissured while one waits for new forms and meanings, should be read as an affirmation of the future to come, of change and possibility. In other words, it is not a matter of a negativity that leads to a paralysis for being or for action. The experience of the impossible means that existence is always expectant, looking toward the horizon, and wagering on what is to come. If being is ontologically open to alterity, to alteration, then action has a revolutionary and creative meaning.

I have already noted that deconstruction is a semiotic interpretation of culture that gives rise to a spectral ontology—though of course the opposite could be said as well, and quite rightly, namely that deconstruction is a spectral ontology that gives rise to a semiotic interpretation of culture. This means that the relation in question is not causal. An ethical problem emerges from this hauntology, which lets us glimpse a limit for action. If being, what is, does not have an ultimate, absolute, and immutable foundation—that is, if it does not rest on firm ground—then there are no criteria according to which the subject can make decisions that lead to right action.[8] However, this limit, this lack of footing, opens as a possibility when we realize, first, that if culture is a semiotic process, then it is also a written text, and, second, that, like all writing, it can be transformed, and transforms itself. This is another instance of overwriting, as in the case of the mystic writing-pad. The subject appears, then, as one more sign in the text; by actively inserting itself into this text, the subject modifies it. The subject thus has the power to transform its cultural context. And from a deconstructive perspective, there *are* criteria for doing so. Or rather, there is at least one very strong criterion, because there is one clear enemy: fascism. Here we should understand fascism in a broad sense, as the effort to totally exclude difference or alterity, where alterity is understood radically as including all that has been repressed, all that has been denied. This repressed other can be thought of as another Dasein, another living thing, nature, another language, another state, another community, and so on.

Deconstruction is an operation that discloses the lack of ontological foundation for all sociopolitical and cultural practices that seek the exclusion and annihilation of the other, of alterity. It is a strategy of interpretation that indicates and denounces efforts to "naturalize" these exclusions. It also sheds light on a reality in which the dominant has been privileged in social, economic, juridical, and cultural terms, and difference has been subordinated, discriminated against, abused, repressed, excluded, and even annihilated.

According to Freud in his interpretation of civilization and its discontents, there is another limit to the political transformation of societies that are ever more inclusive and ever more democratic: the death drive, or the drive to destruction, an inherent tendency in human existence. In *Beyond the Pleasure Principle*, Freud presents the death drive as a tendency that it is impossible to suppress. Nevertheless, this deathly force is always in tension with the life drives. For Freud, human nature is ambivalent; at the same time that it is destructive and antisocial, it is also erotic, a lover of coexistence. From this perspective, it is necessary to think of human existence as a rebellious battle between the life drives and the drives toward destruction.

Here the imperative to go beyond comes into view a bit more clearly.[9] As I noted at the beginning of this introduction, in "Psychoanalysis Searches the States of Its Soul," Derrida proposes the idea of "going beyond the beyond," defined as an unavoidable call to resist cruelty and refuse to fool ourselves when faced with the Freudian discovery of an insuperable drive toward destruction. And in *Beyond*, Freud argues that Eros is another tendency that is also inherent in human nature that manages to interrupt the death drive's movement, to slow down the effects of the drive toward destruction.

The subject of deconstruction is the subject of Freudian psychoanalysis, a subject that, like being, is split and broken apart, caught between Eros and Thanatos. That is, independently of whether or not we take the destructive—and self-destructive—force of the death drive to be insuperable, we must resist. And resistance in deconstruction is not the same as the resistance of Herman Melville's character

Bartleby; it is not a way of saying, "I would prefer not to." It is instead a proactive resistance in the sense that it promotes political activism, denunciation, and the taking of positions.

This is possible because the psyche and human existence are an economy (SE 18: 7), a matter of tension between the forces of Thanatos and those of Eros.[10] Proactive resistance should thus be considered a force that can counter destructive tendencies. To see the reconciliation of differences as a chimerical notion is not to argue for a passive acceptance of war or for an ethics according to which humanity would always be predisposed to recrimination; it is not to give up on the denunciation of all politics that incite violence or discrimination or call on hate.

In 1937, in his text "Analysis Terminable and Interminable," Freud suggests that psychoanalysis is one of three impossible professions. But we should remember that the impossibility of a profession does not imply the cancellation of its character or condition as task; even if the task may be unrealizable, it must be undertaken. The impossibility of these projects is a positive phenomenon that produces effects. This blockage or limit is double-edged: On the one hand, it indicates that inasmuch as there are no absolute truths either in the history of humanity or in the history of the subject, these projects are always aspirations; on the other hand, it indicates that ethically we should proceed with the expectation of change. Such change can be peaceful or disruptive, but closing ourselves off to the irruption of the event inevitably results in the exclusion of difference. Here, then, we find a phenomenological description of the world that discloses an ethical necessity.

The affirmation of antagonism is the only possibility for thinking of a democracy that tends toward inclusion and the erotic. This is precisely what being open to alteration and difference implies: welcoming the other and the modification that the irruption of otherness inescapably entails. But we must underscore the fact that Eros is a tendency and not a form of organization; this means that part of the libido moves toward synthesis without this implying that synthesis is achieved. Eros is movement and not substance. The movement that is open to alteration also translates into a radical ethical position that is valid for all the struggles that humanity fights. Although hauntology circumscribes ontologies of finitude, the limits that it discloses are not uncrossable borders, but rather porous membranes, communicating vessels that allow for mutual modification. This image can, I think, also serve to illustrate the relationship between Eros and Thanatos.

Let us think, for example, of historical forms of discrimination against subjects that differ from the dominant in the juridical terms used to define the latter. In this context, laws must be open to modification because there are always emergent subjects (forms of subjectivity). Here "emergent" can refer to those who have been excluded or those whose forms of life are unprecedented. Structurally, the law must be able to change so that the inclusion of these subjects always remains possible.[11] Any state's constitution must be open to the recognition of new, and old but excluded, forms of subjectivity.

Revolutionary struggles should be fought, even those that are lost in advance. The emergence of new subjectivities and the radical transformation of the world should be morally and ethically accepted. Democracy and justice, for example, should be understood as still pending or suspended, so that the state remains attentive to the necessity of modifying its founding texts. Only in this way can it recognize the need to include rights not previously thought of, or not previously thought to be necessary. This is what it means to say that democracy and justice are to come.

The work of deconstruction shows us a phenomenology out of which an ethics and a politics can be built. That being is not presence, that being is time—this implies, as I have noted, that there are no ultimate, absolute, or immutable ontological foundations. Confronting this phenomenology means calling for an ethics that allows us to think the possibility of changes in meaning. This is what it means to open oneself up to otherness and, even more so, to alteration.

1

The Economy of Alteration

Resistance and Violence

Every limit is a barrier and a point of contact that at once cancels, produces, draws, and originates. Without limits, there would be nothing, and there is nothing without limits. Without limits, we cannot think; the nothing cannot be thought, since thinking's precondition is thinking of the difference between one thing and another. Nevertheless, this difference is not a relation between fully realized identities, not least because identities are not relations. To think of the difference between one thing and another is not a matter of doing violence to the world of multiplicity, with the aim of apprehending fully realized identities; it is instead a matter of treating difference in terms of relation. This new way of thinking of difference turns out to be in fact a way of inhabiting the terrain of paradox and contradiction. I say "inhabiting" and not "thinking" precisely because paradox and contradiction cannot be resolved within a deconstructive framework. If nothing can be thought but limitrophic difference, and this must be thought in terms of relations and not identities, then how can we overcome contradiction? How can we think of limits whose borders are not well defined, borders that imply relations of dependency? Have we not learned that the limit and relation are opposed concepts? What deconstruction discloses, as I will insist throughout this text, is that this impossibility of thinking is one that does not translate into paralysis or inaction, but rather into a radicalization of necessity. This thinking is a form of inhabiting; it at once affirms the urgency of speculative exercise and recognizes its uncertainty and the risk of error. It does not deny the impossibility of thinking in definitive and therefore historical terms. It is precisely what Derrida calls the space of undecidability that thinking of difference in terms of relation opens up; and it is this space that we must inhabit in a way that is not paralyzed but rather politically active. If we do not think the unthinkable, we dwell in the mode of "experience," "smell," "sense," or "apprehension," for example.

To inhabit difference is not to posit an uncrossable boundary between one thing and another, but rather to see limits as lines that touch one another and confound relations of "property." The one and the other belong to one another because difference is always an economic question and a question of degree. That is, there are communicating vessels between one thing and another; the borders between them are porous; the limits separating one thing and another shift; the point that belongs to A then comes to belong to B; and the origin of X is always the alteration of Y. Being is thus an economy of alteration. For this reason, the limit must be thought of as both a barrier and a threshold; if it is the site of resistance to alteration, it at the same time faces the other in a struggle that we could call frontal. The one and the other confront and mirror one another, and their mutual gazing changes both.

What is between the one and the other? What is this limit? "This" thing that "there is" between the one and the other is resistance defined as a force that cares for and conserves the unity of the one and that at the same time pushes outward, affirming itself and in this way altering the other. In this sense, resistance is a force that is as conservative as it is revolutionary. It is the limit that is the origin of the one and the other, but this process is a matter of relations of force that ceaselessly change, because there cannot be two forces with the same intensity, at once different and constant. This would result in a paralysis of being, the end of history, a static time, and a frozen world. As singularities, forces are in constant struggle (involved in collisions) in which their encounter inevitably results in an exchange of quantities. Here again, then, we are dealing with an economy.

Resistance and violence are at the origin. But this phenomenon is not characterized by a linear temporality, where we could give an account of causes and effects. Resistance and violence involve paradoxes. The force that safeguards the one against the other is, for example, violence against the other, but it is also violence against the self, because, as I have already noted, the one cannot exist without the other. The difference between resistance and violence is quantitative. Singularization is the effect of a certain violence against the other, but when the one expels the other, this expulsion leaves traces in both. Thus, the other lives in the one; the one is the other, without this ever resulting in an identity between the two. This identity cannot arise because the one and the other are not fused; they are altered. According to Derrida:

> As soon as there is one, there is murder, wounding, traumatism. *L'Un se garde de l'autre*. The one guards against/keeps some of the other. It *protects* itself from the other, but, in the movement of this jealous violence, it comprises in itself, thus guarding it, the

> self-otherness or self-difference (the difference from within oneself) which makes it One. The "One differing, deferring from itself." The One as the other. At once, at the same time, but in a same time that is out of joint, the One forgets to remember itself to itself, it keeps and erases the archive of this injustice that it is. Of this violence that it does. *L'Un se fait violence*. The One makes itself violence. It violates and does violence to itself but it also institutes itself as violence. It becomes what it is, the very violence—that it does to itself. Self-determination as violence. *L'Un se garde de l'autre pour se faire violence* (because it makes itself violence and *so as* to make itself violence). (*Archive* 78)

In other words, singularization is the effect of a certain violence that acts speculatively, that is, as in a reflection between two mirrors, where the image (here violence) moves ceaselessly between the two sides. The relation between the one and the other is speculative, then, in both senses of the word: as a symmetrical relation of reflection and as a "financial" operation. In economic terms, the result of the difference or differentiation is not pure addition or mere gain; there is something that dies, that is erased, that is lost.

In his long and strange text, the 1895 *Project for a Scientific Psychology*, Freud considers a limit that he thinks of as a membrane that, within a fictitious neurological system, is dedicated to resisting stimulation. In this chapter, I will analyze this limit. The interesting thing about Freud's model is that, in it, it is resistance that gives rise to memory and therefore the psyche, because the Freudian psychic apparatus is a mnemic system. Moreover, it is psychic memory that allows us to explain the phenomenon of "life." The psyche is an apparatus that originates in the struggle between two contradictory tendencies: the pressure to live and the drive to recover an inorganic state. For Freud, the psyche as machine was set in motion at the moment when, according to the myth, the first stimulus, which is always experienced as unpleasure, intruded. In this instant, mechanisms for disposing of the stimulus were also set in motion, even while the stimulus left a mark. This trace was the result of the difference between the organism's force of resistance (let us call it a natural or a priori barrier protecting against the alteration of its exterior) and the force of the stimulation that comes from the world. In this way, the inscription left open a path that would lead to the discharging of unpleasure, but this also means that the route leading to relief became longer. The mark is thus a mnemic trace archive, one that delays death without overcoming it. In this model, life, the psyche, and memory become words that are not synonymous but can be used interchangeably.

Freud's *Project* seeks "to furnish us with a psychology which shall be a natural science: that is, to represent psychical processes as quantitatively determinate states of specifiable material particles, thus making those processes perspicuous and free from contradiction" (SE 1: 295). Despite the extravagance of this objective, and the fact that, as Freud noted to his friend and alter ego Wilhelm Fliess, he put the *Project* in a box and did not want anything more to do with it, this manuscript lays out the design and description of a brilliant model of the psyche, one that in a veiled way (but a way that is evident to a committed reader of Freud) will accompany him throughout all of his psychoanalytic writings that center on the functioning and outlines of the psychic apparatus. Fundamentally, the problem that Freud addresses in the *Project*—and that he will continue to approach in important texts that include Letter 52 (to Fliess), the seventh chapter of *The Interpretation of Dreams*, *Beyond the*

Pleasure Principle, and "A Note Upon the Mystic Writing-Pad"—is one of the guiding problems for all psychoanalytic theory: How is it possible that the same apparatus fulfills two mutually exclusive functions, the function of perception and that of memory, at the same time? How can the psyche function as an archive, seemingly without end, while at the same time remaining open to ever more new information? In other words, this was a matter of resolving the enigma of a "multitasking" mind, with a perception-consciousness system and a mnemic system that was itself further fragmented, because, as Derrida observes in *Archive Fever,* there are two registers within the mnemic system, one mnemic and one hypomnemic. The latter contains repressed unconscious material that does not become present to consciousness except in order to outmaneuver it and produce distorted forms. The hypomnemic register is paradoxically a memory that is "forgotten," although of course "forgetting" in psychoanalysis cannot be understood as something defenseless, petrified, or innocuous, because what is forgotten and repressed, for Freud, is always active and tends toward the perception-consciousness system in order to lead the action that would satisfy desire. Resistances are the work of unconscious thought that seeks to keep repressed material forgotten; this effort represents a great expenditure of energy for the psychic organization, and it is this that in mental "illness" is experienced as malaise, discontent, or suffering.

Freud begins the description of the psychic apparatus by making a distinction between perception and the mnemic system, setting the problem of repression aside in order to return to it later in the text. The model of the psychic apparatus in this set of notes is a sort of neurological fiction that centers on two (later three) different types of neurons, which are said to sustain the two fundamental (and mutually exclusive) functions of the psychic apparatus, that is, perception and memory, designated as ϕ and ψ, respectively. Freud explains that these two neurons are not structurally differentiated, but rather differentiated exclusively in quantitative terms, that is, specifically in terms of the quantity of resistance that their "contact-barriers" offer against the passage of energy. ϕ neurons, or neurons of perception, offer practically no resistance; by contrast, ψ neurons, or neurons of memory, do offer resistance. The latter are the neurons that form a mnemic archive, and the shock of the encounter between the resistance that they impose, on the one hand, and, on the other, the force of the irruption of the stimulus opens a path—a channel—through which the next excitations to the apparatus will be diffused. What is interesting here is that, with each recurrence, these paths become ever more passable until they become, according to Freud, ϕ neurons. This means that the psyche, as a mnemic machine, is led inevitably and inherently toward death defined as a debilitation, a weakening of the resistance that defers discharge. The resistance of the contact-barriers thus fulfills two functions that must not be thought of as contradictory: retains and dissipates, disappears, or disperses.

For Freud, as he describes it in "A Note Upon the Mystic Writing-Pad," memory is a trace understood as writing. (And this is not only true of the "Note"; although he does not specifically refer to writing, it is clear in the *Project for a Scientific Psychology*, Letter 52, and Chapter 7 of *The Interpretation of Dreams* as well as in *Beyond the Pleasure Principle* that memory is a matter of inscription.) But it should be clear that writing is possible if and only if there is "resistance to writing." According to Freud, an organization—whether psychic or what we could call "pre-psychic"—"naturally" offers a certain quantity of energy as a resistance to stimulation, and it is the shock of the encounter between this repulsion and the force of the stimulus that results in an inscription.

Later, mnemic inscriptions make up a sort of furrowed terrain that the drive must cross in order to discharge stimuli, and the course of this writing delays the achievement of the drive's aim. Thus resistance is the origin of psychic life (and of life in general, according to the Freudian mythology), and psychic life is the effect of writing, defined as a mnemic archive that gives rise to an erotic detour before death.

In the *Project*, facilitation, which accounts for the psychic process of memory, is a writing made of traces. Facilitation, defined as the opening of a passage, is a sort of piercing. The German word that Freud uses for this process is *Bahnung*, which has been translated into English as facilitation and into Spanish as *facilitación*. In Strachey's translation:

> It will be well now to clear our mind as to what assumptions about the ψ-neurones [neurons of memory] are necessary in order to cover the most general characteristics of memory. This is the argument. They are permanently altered by the passage of an excitation. If we introduce the theory of contact-barriers: their contact-barriers are brought into a permanently altered state. And since psychological knowledge shows that there is such a thing as a re-learning on the basis of memory, this alteration must consist in the contact-barriers becoming more capable of conduction, less impermeable, and so more like those of the ϕ system. We shall describe this condition of the contact-barriers as their degree of *facilitation* [*Bahnung*]. We can then say: *Memory is represented by the facilitations existing between the ψ neurones*. (SE 1: 300; emphasis in original)

In his English translation of Derrida's "Freud and the Scene of Writing," Alan Bass translates *Bahnung* as "breaching," and in his Spanish translation, Patricio Peñalver translates it as *apertura de paso*, the opening of a passage.[1] This latter translation comes closer to the neuronal model that Freud proposes in the *Project*. The image to which *Bahnung* refers is closer to the opening of a path or, according to Derrida's reading, the tracing of a furrow, than to the "facilitation" of the transmission of energy. Luiz Hanns's *Diccionario de términos alemanes de Freud* (Dictionary of Freud's German Terms) says that "the noun *Bahn* evokes the image of a 'path' or 'walkable trail.' The noun *Bahnung* is a nominalization of the act of 'creating a path,' 'excavating,' 'installing,' 'opening' a walkable trail." Hanns also says that "a *Bahn* is first of all something flat and horizontal, the trail over which one 'slides' or through which one 'passes' easily. *Bahnung* is therefore something that is installed on the terrain of a difficult topography" (266–267). I see two main problems with the choice of "facilitation" or *facilitación* as a translation of *Bahnung*. First, this translation does not refer to the "permanent alteration" of the contact-barriers of the ψ neurons that, for Freud, is fundamental to the psychic process of memory. Thinking in terms of the opening of a passage, however, does allow us to recover this sense. *Facilitation*, according to the *Oxford English Dictionary*, refers to making an action possible, making the achievement of an end easy, or promoting or assisting with something. These meanings generate confusion and lead to erroneous interpretations, because in Freud memory is not exclusively a matter of making the transmission of energy possible. Rather, the fundamental thing about the phenomenon of memory is the alteration of the contact-barrier that the repetition of excitation provokes. This is what the image of the opening of a passage or the tracing of a furrow allows us easily to recuperate, and what Freud refers to when he says "that there is such a thing as a re-learning on the basis of memory" (SE 1: 300). Second, the opening of a passage, of a path, or the tracing of a furrow also allows us to recover the violence that *Bahnung* implies, for Freud. The furrow that is opened responds to the difficulty of marking or of inscription given the resistance or defense that the psychic apparatus mounts, in keeping with what we could call its nature. The opening of such a road always implies difficulty and violence.

In addition, the image of opening a passage or a path also refers to the connection between two elements, a connection not retained in the idea of facilitation. According to Hanns:

> In Spanish the term [*facilitación*, like the English "facilitation"] does not evoke anything related to "the physical interconnection between two elements"; nor does it highlight the dynamic element of flow or linkage. It refers to a process of removing obstacles, a removal that "facilitates" access. Overall, the use of this term is more figurative or metaphorical, referring to obstacles or forms of access that are abstract. It does not have *Bahnung*'s concrete quality. (268)

The origin of the psyche, of memory, and of life is thus the resistance of the ψ neurons, the force that their borders offer against alteration. This is a paradoxical movement in which the resistance to alteration produces a mark that will delay death. In *Beyond the Pleasure Principle*, Freud opens with the following claim:

> In the theory of psycho-analysis of the mind we have no hesitation in assuming that the course taken by mental events is automatically regulated by the pleasure principle. We believe, that is to say, that the course of those events is invariably set in motion by an unpleasurable state of tension, and that it takes a direction such that its final outcome coincides with

> a lowering of that tension—that is, with an avoidance of unpleasure or a production of pleasure. (SE 18: 7)

This means that the principle that will rule over psychic life will be one that tends toward death, because the total discharge of stimulation is nothing other than a return to an inanimate state. Life is a quantity of discomfort or, in metapsychological terms, a surcharge of stimulation.

Here I would like to open a parenthesis to call attention to the *foreign* nature of stimulation, to the fact that what occupies the psyche and what the psyche seeks to ward off arrives from an organism that is other or, at least, experienced as alien. The extravagance of psychic life (and of life in general) derives from the fact that by resisting alteration and seeking to expel what alters it, the psyche brings about a mark, a trace that is always remembered. This trace is writing, and is writing because it is a mark, as Derrida brilliantly notes. The paradox, then, is fundamentally that this is a detour that is not an overcoming. Life does not overcome death; it only postpones it. As the *Project* recounts, the stimulus manages to pass through or to be discharged in the paths of the ϕ neurons without encountering any opposition, that is, without leaving a trace. The opposite happens with ψ neurons, because their contact-barriers offer a force of resistance that, when it encounters an external stimulus, gives rise to writing. This inscription is now a supplemental path to be traveled, a detour that will delay discharge and defer death. The detour is thus life itself. In short, memory is a map of the cratered surface that complicates and stands in the way of the short-circuiting of death.

Memory responds to the difference between two itineraries, that is, the difference between two resistances, two different paths opened and there to be "chosen."[2] Without a passage, a path, open before it, memory would be paralyzed.

Recall how, in the *Project*, the contact-barriers of the ψ neurons are not all "equally well facilitated" and do not "offer[] equal resistance" (SE 1: 300). Freud explains that this difference among facilitations is what gives rise to memory. Memory is thus nothing other than the difference between distinct open passages. It is a psychic map of the furrows that have been created, through which the psyche's alteration by the world will be channeled.

Therefore *polemos*, defined as difference, as a battle between distinct forces, is the origin, although, according to Derrida, in the terms of the metaphysics of presence, a difference cannot be an original principle. Nevertheless, we can say that this is an origin under erasure or crossed out, an ~~origin~~, since singularity stems from violence, although without bringing the movement of its displacements or changes in value to a halt.

The *Project*'s model of the psyche treats membranes as contact-barriers, as borders between distinct organisms or organizations. What I would like to emphasize is that this neurological fiction can serve to help us think, and that it can complicate not only the problem of memory, but also the borders between nations, and more specifically the quantity of resistance that can or should be offered against the foreign. For example, the question might be formulated in this way: Is it borders, defined as sites of resistance, in any of its forms, that are the ~~origin~~ of multiplicity? In political and ethical-political terms, multiplicity is not only desirable and acceptable; it must be respected, promoted, and cultivated. Why, then, do we on the left like John Lennon's song "Imagine" so much? Have we really imagined a world without countries, without borders? Yes, of course, the song is inspiring and heartwarming, and of course it makes us smile, but have we thought through the consequences of the world for which it calls? Wouldn't its vision lead to the disappearance of all differences, making us all one? The anthem even says it: "And the world will be as one." This is not the most benign vision for those of us who dream, together with Lennon, of a world in which there would be no more ideologies or religions to kill or die for. It would seem instead that a certain resistance to difference, even a certain violence, is and will be, paradoxically, necessary for the cultivation of differences.

When Freud calls on us to remain vigilant lest we revert to the "narcissism of minor differences" (SE 21: 114), we should thus think in terms of degree, in terms of quantitative differences that of course imply differences in quality, but not in terms of essential differences. Curiously, this is the question that Freud asks in the *Project* when he realizes that his energetic model does not account for the perception of attributes, that is, for the fact that our senses are not only responsive to quantities of force; in an immediate way, stimuli are translated into the qualities of color, taste, size, stridency, harmony, smell, and so on. It is at this point in his discussion that Freud introduces ω or W-neurons, charged with the task of completing this translation. It will be the periodicity of stimulation, or the rhythm of excitation and its interruption, that will allow for the passage from quantity to quality.

The violence of borders or political limits can and must, I think, also be thought of in quantitative terms. Although certain degrees of violence cannot be overcome, when we realize that in violence there is still the possibility of giving space to difference defined as plurality in multiplicity, the ethical-political problem is magnified exponentially. This is because the danger of resistance can at the same time be annihilation or the possibility of annihilating. What we call cultural differences can survive only if there is a certain resistance to alteration, but, at the same time the "narcissistic" danger of overvaluing the endogenous has tended, and still tends, to produce damaging consequences, terrible exclusions, and even extinctions, or, to spell it out, fascism. The problem thus leads us to the question of authority, that is: Who decides who deserves to survive and who does not? Who decides how to resist and how much resistance there should be?

How and when do we take in the foreign, and how much foreignness do we take in? What can we, and what can we not, ask the guest to give up, to renounce? These questions arise when "one" is foreign: What renunciations can we ask of the host, when we are the ones who barge into another organism? It is not the purpose of this text to respond in detail to all of these questions, because my interest in this context is only to point to the problematic. Nevertheless, I think it is important not to lose sight of the fact that, whatever specific response we might give to these questions, it will have a shaky ground, or mud, as its foundation. In other words, there are no laws, universal or even "universalizable" rules, with which the One can locate itself, or one can locate oneself, in general terms. The conflicts between the one and the other should, and can only, be resolved by thinking in terms of singularity, accounting for specific contexts or circumstances. The foreigner, the guest, the one who renounces, the quantity and character of resistance or of alteration—all must have specific features in order for a "resolution" to approach (because it will only approach) justice. Justice, as Derrida rightly says, in order to carry that exalted name, must be singular, must be an event. It necessarily brings creativity and plasticity together in order to produce what we might call a harmonious rhythm of resistance and alteration that in turn leads to lower degrees of violence. In the end, the one and the other, paradoxically, can only survive if they engage in this sort of dance, in which the erotic bears the mark of certain extinction and death opens the space for new forms of life.

Borders are membranes at the beginning (understood as origins) and in the end (understood as sites of extinction). Not all novelty is desirable, and not all erasure is reprehensible. Free passage between membranes would therefore be a political action worth promoting, but the same would not be true of the wholesale disappearance of membranes as such, or of what we could call tissues of limitation. Although the lack of universal criteria causes anguish, we can conversely think of this lack as promising, as hopeful, because it opens the possibility of emancipation, if we bear in mind that alteration can transform politics, knowledge, and repressive practices as well.

The result of the difference between resistance and alteration is, according to Derrida—and Freud, or according to Derrida following Freud—writing. But let us go further and say that the essence of writing is its openness to the future and what is to come. Writing is always open to overwriting. This must be understood as an "essential capacity for modification." Here the writing that we must think of is not the writing produced by the application of ink to a piece of paper, but rather something more like the effect of tracing a path in the ground. The difference between the forces of resistance and those of alteration produces an inscription. It is necessary to think in terms of furrows because they are always susceptible to changes in shape. In ethical-political terms, subjects' actions have the power to modify everything that we think of as "already written," including especially the law. I refer to the law because we cannot simply place faith in the prudence and altruism of the members of our species.

The subject has the power to transform its cultural context. In ethical terms, the subject must take on this power and think of itself as an agent whose action is revolutionary. It must act—in fact, it acts, whether voluntarily or involuntarily, since the refusal to act also has effects—even knowing that there is no certainty about the consequences of its actions. But the claim that there are no universal criteria should not be taken to mean that there are no criteria at all. The criterion instead becomes a sort of compass that is always accompanied by the specter of error. Paradoxically, only such an equivocal guide for action can help us to approach justice. It is a matter, then, of weak criteria that are not for all that unsound.

What is fundamental in all of this is that, in general, the force of resistance must be less than the force of the other that produces alteration, as long as—and here the generalization is inevitably qualified—the force that breaks through does not seek to annihilate the one, or unless this force is a fascist force in the broad sense, that is, a demand for the exclusion of difference or otherness, where the latter is defined radically as all that has been repressed or disavowed.

If resistance is so forceful that it does not allow (to continue to think in terms of writing) for the other's inscription, then the result is a condition that remains unchanged, and an exclusion has therefore taken place. We thus have to ask whether a resistance that is greater than the force that irrupts or breaks in can still be thought of as resistance or should be referred to using another name. Resistance is not blockage; it is not isolation; it is not impermeability. Isolation can be understood as a kind of destitution or orphanhood. It is for all of these reasons that the force of resistance must be less than the force of the alien or foreign. An impenetrable border—or one whose crossing can become the cause of death, as in the case of the "Border" between the United States and Mexico, or, lest we forget, that between Mexico and Guatemala—is not a membrane that resists, but rather a wall that violently contains. We can go further and think of the result of exclusion or annihilation, which is always autoimmune. A lack of solicitation results in an absence of excitation, and thus if, as I noted earlier, life can be understood as an effort to be rid of alteration and regain a certain equilibrium or constancy, then refusing entry to a given quantity can be the end of life.

We are dealing with the fundamental paradox for life and survival. First, the one needs to oppose the other with a certain force, because otherwise, without this opposition, the other would supplant the one. But second—although this is really the same phenomenon—the opposition must be of a magnitude that allows for the "economized" passage of the other, since the one, as we have seen, is "nourished," fed by, the other. That is, nothing is one if there is no other, because in this ecosystem there can be no radical self-sustainability. The survival of singularity depends on this difference; it thus hinges on the call of the other, which is multiple. If the resistance to alteration is equal to or greater than the force that would exceed it (here equal and greater resistance both lead to the same result), then there is no life. There is nothing. According to Freud, life is a drive to be rid of alteration, of the other, and to sustain the one—to bear it to death, to be sure, but this route is a detour to be traveled, a circuitous path, an erotic parenthesis, a creative interval. (All of this can, of course, be deathly, but I want to emphasize the possibility that the journey along this path can itself be complicated, rather than leading in a straight and direct line toward death. The erotic journey is also ecological in the sense that more than one organism can share the same space-time within it.)

Eros should not be thought of as pure life. Eros is *bios*,[3] because it is always already the good life, or a life marked by politics, by justice, that is, by the other. This tendency is marked by the reality principle, defined as a modification of the pleasure principle that manages to delay death. Eros does not overcome death but does not rush toward it either. Inhabiting the world erotically implies a recognition of and complicity with the other; it thus implies complexity of the kind produced by compound organisms. Eros is not another name for Nirvana, because it is a force of conflict or *polemos* that gives rise to the unprecedented. The detour that Freud describes in *Beyond the Pleasure Principle* and that he names "the reality principle" is the path that the one takes together with the other; it implies a turn toward the social, toward the common, and therefore toward politics, economy, and justice.

Still, Eros does not overcome death. And so? Why bother with life, with the bother that is life? We should not forget that the source of this disturbance is, in precise Freudian terms, the excitation of the foreign or what exceeds the one. So how can we think this paradox, in which Eros at once bypasses death and is led inevitably toward it? Freud's response to this question is, on the one hand, scandalously close to Heidegger and, on the other hand, atypically poetic. He says: "The organism wishes to die only in its own fashion" (SE 18: 39). In other words, the psyche does not kill itself, does not lead the organism to the short-circuit of death, because it wants to design its own death, and this deathly architecture passes through others and through the world in general. It would seem that Freud might say that the social revolves fundamentally around respect for the intimate regulation of one's own death.

By this account, life would be a way of "economizing" the irruption or intrusion of the other, something like a calculus that would allow one to avoid the annihilation of singularity, of the one. But, at the same time, this would not imply a blockage that would leave the one unaltered or identical.

Derrida names this phenomenon life death noting that life and death are not distinct phenomena that stand opposed to one another, each identical to itself, but rather one sole phenomenon in which two tendencies mirror one another in an infinite game of reflection that has the effect of producing a relation of sameness. The paradox of life death is resolved by the death of the organism, but resistance to alteration and the setting to work of mechanisms for avoiding excitation form the parenthesis in which both singularities, life and death, emerge. Because only what is living dies; only the living is led toward death. Life and finitude originate in one and the same instant. For Derrida, this phenomenon is an autoimmune disease; it is, he says, an archive fever. And the parenthesis of life is necessarily an archive, a store of excitations of which the organism cannot rid itself immediately. We should not overlook the fact that this storage can only originate in the threat of death. In other words, infinity does not allow for reserves. According to Derrida:

> *On the one hand*, the archive is made possible by the death, aggression, and destruction drive, that is to say also by originary finitude and expropriation. But beyond finitude as limit, there is . . . this properly *infinite* movement of radical destruction without which no archive desire or fever would happen. (*Archive Fever* 94; emphases in original)

This "fever" or evil [*mal*] that, as Derrida indicates in the quotation above, has elements of radical annihilation, gives rise, in the very instant of its genesis, to the production of antibodies, but it never leads to the creation of an antidote. Life is therefore an economy of evil [*mal*] in the sense that it seeks to delay death. "Archive fever" [*el mal de archivo*] refers to what is inherent in every process or technique of archivization and operates according to a logic of self-destruction, because "anarchiving destruction belongs to the process of archivization and produces the very thing it reduces" (*Archive Fever* 94).

Membranes, understood as limits between the one and the other, are permeable, and in ethical-political terms they have to be permeable for reasons that are both selfish and altruistic. But what archive fever discloses is that at the end of history, everything will disappear. History can be drawn out for as long as one likes, and unities can be defined as either complex or as simple, but what is certain is that the one as singularity is driven toward its own annihilation. This phenomenon can be understood as a matter of what doctors call "internal causes," but these causes are in fact undecidably both internal and external. I noted earlier that the survival of every organism depends on its interaction or exchange with other organisms; the world is an ecosystem and a very complex one. But it is true that each instant of interaction implies a transformation in which something is gained and at the same time something is lost, or fades and dies. Life is a history of alterations and is therefore at the same time a history of death.

Freud's model of the psyche reveals this autoimmune condition in a paradigmatic way. In the neurological fiction of Freud's *Project*, for example, the process of pathbreaking or facilitation shows how the alteration of contact-barriers is also a weakening of these barriers that tends toward their overcoming or defeat. In a retrospective reading of this text in light of Freud's "discovery" of the death drive twenty years later, we can see that the death drive works on each new discharge by modifying the resistance of the ψ neurons. In fact, according to this Freudian model, the neurons that are impermeable (ψ) aspire to the condition of those that are permeable (ϕ). In Freud's words, the ψ neurons

> are permanently altered by the passage of an excitation. If we introduce the theory of contact-barriers: their contact-barriers are brought into a permanently altered state. And since psychological knowledge shows that there is such a thing as a re-learning on the basis of memory, this alteration must consist in the contact-barriers becoming more capable of conduction, less impermeable, and so more like those of the ϕ system. (SE 1: 300)

This process corresponds, in fact, to facilitation. In this way, the construction of a reserve, archive, or memory finally serves to fulfill the primary function—the function that tends toward discharge, or the death of the psychic apparatus—because the system of neurons saves the quantities of stimulation that lead to the creation of facilitations.

It is true that memory offers an opportunity to delay death, but death is always an imminent possibility; it can happen without announcing itself in advance. As Derrida says, it is not that "death surprises life. It founds memory" ("Freud and the Scene of Writing," in *Writing and Difference* 228). On the other hand, all reserves are finite:

> All psychical acquisition would in that case consist in the organization of the ψ system through partial and locally determined lifting of the resistance in the contact-barriers which distinguishes ϕ and ψ. With the advance of this organization the nervous system's capacity for fresh reception would literally have reached a barrier. (SE 1: 302)

This is the limit of the psychic apparatus, its death. It is therefore memory that discloses the play of forces between life and death. It is also memory that shows us that the difference between these two forces accounts for the fact that life is a detour rather than a direct and immediate path to death.

The singular organism that we have treated here, and the psyche that Freud describes in terms that we could call intimate, contrasting it with something more like a social psyche, can also be thought of as a nation. The question might therefore be posed in the following terms: How are we to take in the foreigner? If a nation were to function metaphorically as a psyche, it would ideally be surrounded by membranes that were permeable to foreigners, rather than uncrossable borders. If these were membranes understood as limits and not as points of access or entry without resistance, then we would have to ask ourselves if one can gain access, can accede, to that which does not resist. I do not think so. It seems to me that the notion of access implies another space that naturally has limits, since a space cannot be thought of without these. But let us continue to elaborate the metaphor. What is a hospitable nation? John Lennon's utopia of love, taken to the point of absurdity, would turn the world into a place full of zombies, a place where no one is called or solicited, no one is insulted, everyone understands everyone else, and everything is translated or translatable. In such a place, differences would evaporate; there would be no life because there would be no memory.

Hospitality should be unconditional, as Derrida notes, because we are obligated to respect the rights of the visitor, among many others. But hospitality is another paradoxical political phenomenon. First of all, there is only a guest if there is a host, that is, if in some way the space that will be shared has been occupied and delimited beforehand by the one who opens her doors. This delimitation fundamentally implies particular laws that the guest is at the very least invited to respect, but that in the majority of cases this guest is obligated to observe. Second, however, we cannot speak of hospitality without also speaking of respect for the rules, laws, habits, or customs of the new place of residence. There is no way of finding welcome or being hosted in a place where all foreignness or extravagance is punished or abolished. But another qualification is necessary, because not all kinds of "extravagance" entail the same consequences. For example, it would not be desirable, under any circumstances or in any context, if clitoridectomy were permitted in any part of Mexico. How do we welcome the foreigner, then? I have said unconditionally, but this is not and cannot be quite true. Without borders we cannot even speak of hospitality. It would seem, then, that there is no psychic hospitality, to return to our metaphor, in permeable (ϕ) neurons. Where there is no resistance, there is no reception, no one who receives or takes in anyone else. Permeable neurons do not produce memory and therefore do not create life. They do not create anything.

All borders should therefore resemble ψ neurons, that is, they should offer a certain amount of resistance, to be sure. But here we should insist that this resistance must always be much less forceful than the force that it opposes, because otherwise there would be no mnemic trace or hospitality for the foreigner. We should think of the borders between nations, or more generally of borders between the one and the other, as resembling impermeable (ψ) neurons, which are always altered by external stimulation. Because the irruption or intrusion of the foreign should always allow for the modification of the host. Otherwise, there is no writing in Derrida's sense. (Remember that this is a trace, a matter of creating furrows, new paths, texts, channels of discharge, or paths for transit.) There is no memory and therefore no life, because, as I noted at the beginning of this chapter, life is nothing other than the tendency to try to be rid of stimulation from without, from the foreign. Hence the paradox of life, which cannot exist without the other but at the same time aims to annul it. In other words, it is the other that founds life rather than inhibits it.

In ethical and political terms, on the one hand, we can see the necessity of engaging in what Derrida (in "Eating Well") calls a kind of calculus between conservatism (always moderate, of course) and liberalism (always excessive, obviously). Only the resistance offered by a permeable membrane can be moderately conservative and at the same time liberally excessive. Since our resistance to the foreigner must be less than the force of her arrival, this implies that the nation is (and must be) open to modification. I am not only referring to its culture, language, and cuisine, where syncretism is always desirable; I also mean its Magna Carta, because in order for a constitution to give rise to democracy and justice, the state must always remain open to the necessity of its reform. Only in this way can the process of inclusion, the extension of rights that were previously unthinkable or unnecessary, become permanent. This is the permanent revolution of which Maurice Blanchot speaks, the revolution that breaks open the connection between permanence and substantial presence (Derrida, *Specters* 39–40).

2

The Economy of Sacrifice

Melancholic Elaborations

The central argument of Freud's *Totem and Taboo*, a work of social psychoanalysis — or if not the text's main argument, then its essential narrative — is that the social order is born from and sustained by two prohibitions that rule out the satisfaction of two desires: the incestuous and the cannibalistic. Totemic societies regulate these prohibitions economically.[1] Freud offers the hypothesis that before these taboos were established, there was no social organization, and human beings were grouped into "hordes": "The totem meal, which is perhaps mankind's earliest festival, would thus be a repetition and commemoration of this memorable and criminal deed with which was the beginning of so many things — of social organization, of moral restrictions, and of religion" (SE 13: 142). Thus civilized human beings are exogamous when it comes to both sex and food. But paradoxically Freud suspects, and offers as a strong and plausible hypothesis, that human community is founded on the secret (repression) of a scene that transgresses one of these two laws (although perhaps when we refer to this point in history it is incorrect to speak of transgressions, since prohibitions had not yet been laid down). In the beginning, a patricidal crime was committed, and a cannibal feast followed. The primal horde killed and then devoured the father. The second fundamental and foundational moment is the moment of shared responsibility; this second moment is the place of a cut in the historical process, and it marks, for Freud, the event in which civilization originates. Beyond the murder and ingestion of the father, we find the complicity among brothers, where Freud locates the possibility of a "social contract." In other words, it is because the crime was committed by a group that the collective resists, protects itself, and is immortalized:

> Society was now based on complicity in the common crime; religion was based on the sense of guilt and the remorse attaching to it; while morality was based partly on the exigencies of this society and partly on the penance demanded by the sense of guilt. (SE 13: 146)

In the Freudian myth recounting the origin of civilization, there are thus at least three stages. First, in a state of nature, human beings were incestuous and cannibalistic. Second, in the order that was established on the basis of the economic regulation of incestuous and cannibalistic desires, this paradoxically gave rise to the murder of the father by the primal horde or band of brothers, who ate the father they had killed. Third and finally, a social contract was established that fundamentally prohibited the satisfaction of these two appetites, incestuous and cannibalistic. Nevertheless, the key fact about this third stage is that the social contract only became possible because, on the one hand, the brothers were complicit in having committed the crime, and, on the other hand, the social order protected the brothers' lives on these two conditions: They would not eat one another, and sexual intercourse with the women in the horde was ruled out. In other words, the social contract could sustain and preserve itself only on the basis of shared guilt and the democratization of sexual intercourse through a universal prohibition on endogamy. This means that the social demand for exogamy originates in an effort to prevent the envy that might arise if some were afforded privileged and incestuous access to the female members of the group. Didn't Horkheimer and Adorno also say that envy is the force that moves the world? It would seem that they were not mistaken.

But let us insist on another node in this account of the origin of the social order: secrecy. The history of civilization has kept the secret of these two crimes, which Freud offers as both a hypothesis and a necessary speculative deduction: One day in the history of *homo sapiens*, these crimes must have been committed, because otherwise they would not have left so many traces in history and in the psyche both collective and individual.[2]

In the effort to understand the origin and conservation of the social order, the crime committed is as important as repressed memory of this crime, that is, its negation, which makes it endure permanently in the unconscious. Let us not forget that the radical hypothesis that Freud offers in *Totem and Taboo* is that these prohibitions arise because incestuous and cannibalistic desires are inherent in human nature. The argument here is very simple: Without these desires, there would be no need for the prohibitions.

For Freud, the unconscious is always pulsating, a force that constantly seeks to assert itself in the world. The unconscious is a source of excitation that seeks only discharge. Incestuous and cannibalistic desires are permanent pulsations, and the ban on their satisfaction thus cannot be once and done; it must be repeated. The prohibition must repeat itself compulsively in laws, institutions, languages, and all apparatuses of authority. Isn't it here that we can locate the genesis of the phylogenetic inheritance that binds us to a sense of responsibility for these criminal desires? Aren't all of these authoritarian apparatuses symptoms of our need to prevent and repress the irruption of these desires?

Derrida writes in *The Gift of Death* that the history of the West is a history of murders, of shared secrets, complicities, and common denials. Yes, the history of civilization is the history of a series of crimes committed "for the common good"; because the latter is "good" and "common," we do not call the crimes committed for its sake by their names. We disavow the sacrifice of what is "bad," of "evil," and so on. For psychoanalysis, disavowal is a defense mechanism that is distinguished from negation in that the unwanted material is not relegated to the unconscious; disavowal involves living "as if one didn't know" when in fact one does know. Asked directly about this knowledge, the subject "in denial" responds, "Yes, yes, I know."[3] To sacrifice what is bad—or, in the case of the primal horde in the Freudian myth, to sacrifice the sovereign male—for the sake of democratization turns out to be an alibi that claims to be for "the common good," or for the "good of the community."

Civilization and culture are sustained by the repetition of sacrifices that, even when they do not involve bloodshed, do not cease to be marked by a certain cruelty. What, for example, is the death penalty? Isn't it scandalous that in the United States some defend this form of punishment on grounds that it does not involve bloodshed?[4] Why isn't "lethal injection" also cruel? Wasn't the Nazis' use of gas chambers cruel? In "Psychoanalysis Searches the States of Its Soul," Derrida highlights, on the one hand, the Latin derivation of the term *cruelty*, which is inseparably linked to the idea of bloodshed, and, on the other, the word's affiliation with the German *Grausamkeit*, which Freud uses. The latter word, without necessarily involving bloodshed, names the desire to "make . . . suffer *just to* suffer, even to torture or to kill; to kill oneself or torture oneself to torture or kill, *just to* take a psychic pleasure in evil for evil's sake, or even *just to* find bliss in radical evil" (238–239; emphasis in original). According to Derrida: "One can staunch bloody cruelty (*cruor, crudus, crudelitas*), one can put an end to murder by blade, by the guillotine, in the classical or modern theaters of bloody war, but according to Nietzsche or Freud, a psychic cruelty will always take its place by inventing new resources" ("Psychoanalysis Searches" 239). This is precisely the problem that I seek to address in this chapter, a problem confronted not only by pacifist political philosophy, but by politics itself, that is, cruelty understood as inherent in human nature and thus as an insuperable limit.

The social order or the order of the common not only originates here; it also maintains itself and is reaffirmed here, in the infinite and compulsive repetition of the everyday sacrifice of our body, the most pulsating, desiring body, one as deathly as it is erotic. In the terms of a psychoanalytic economy, the civilized subject is nothing other than the subject that has managed to turn the pleasure principle into the reality principle. We should not forget that the reality principle does not work against the pleasure principle but rather for it; that is, it does not require a renunciation of pleasure, only a delay, a satisfaction that is saved for later. But this is the ideal subject; the subject we might call fanatical is one that does not manage to complete this economic transaction successfully and so sets countless psychic mechanisms in motion in an effort to suffocate desire. But added to this is the fact that desire is insuperable and inescapable; it cannot be extinguished, and even the majority of defense mechanisms add fuel to its fire, leading to incendiary neurosis.

The subject, defined as that region of the psyche produced by the incorporation of the law, the other, and culture, can never catch up with all of its desires, and what has not been subjected is the always rebellious unconscious and the id.

Couldn't we therefore think of the ego, the subject, what has been subjected, as the effect of sacrifice? The ego is not what is sacrificed; it is instead the agent of sacrifice. The ego is, in this sense, a criminal. The ego, like Abraham (the Father of faith), is the one who hears the call of the faceless other, of otherness as institution, law, and authority that not only has no definite face, but has many confounding features. The ego is the effect of the sacrifice of the desiring body, a sacrifice that is compulsively repeated. The desiring body is, according to this analogy, Isaac, but there is no lamb. When it comes to these sacrifices—the sacrifice of one's own body and of others' bodies—doesn't Freud say in *Totem and Taboo*, that life in society and in communities is sustained by the regulation of sex and eating? The fundamental and foundational taboos prohibit certain sexual relations and the ingestion of certain foods; they prohibit incestuous endogamy and cannibalism. (It is true that every state and almost every religion then more specifically defines exogamy and the diet that will bring together the community or allow for the avoidance of evil.) In fact, during the whole history of what we call civilization, these two prohibitions have not undergone any modification. Belonging to a community is conditional on these two prohibitions. On the one hand, no crimes generate more fear than those that transgress these laws; on the other hand, the subject subjected to the law, to the law defined as the most common thing we have, is the effect of the sacrifice of these savage and primitive desires.

According to this way of thinking, the ego is the site of the general within the singular; the ego is what is subjected to norms, the effect of the incorporation of the community's laws. The ego is the agency that responds in advance, and its response is always a reflection of the other's call. The ego is the place of responsibility for everything in the other that exceeds the body. The ego is all of us in our singularity. But do we not confront a dramatic paradox here? Isn't *ego* ("I" in Latin) a singular grammatical subject? In this context, in terms of the mind-body dichotomy, the body of the drives [*el cuerpo pulsivo*] would instead be the radically singular, that which does not respond and is not responsible, because it is a force, and force only seeks to affirm itself, in and of itself. On the other hand, we cannot deny that the ego is at the same time the site of differentiation between inside and outside. But the singularity of every ego must be thought of as the unrepeatable result (and here another economy appears) of a transaction between the world, radical otherness, and each living, "unclonable" body or organism.[5] The ego would thus be what remains, what is left of the negotiation or encounter between the forces of the outside and the force of bodily desire that seeks to affirm itself in the world, over and above the other. Nevertheless, if it is the ego that responds, it responds to the call of the law of the other, of the world; it thus cannot be thought of as the site or support of singularity. The ego is therefore also undecidable, in that we cannot render a single and verifiable decision as to whether it is singular or plural. We can only say that the ego is what responds, before a community, on behalf of an irresponsible body.

In the very apt meeting of the minds that Judith Butler stages in *The Psychic Life of Power*, which brings together Nietzsche, Hegel, Althusser, Foucault, and Freud, we can identify the thread that connects and binds these thinkers. This is the idea, shared by all of them, that the subject is the effect of a turning in on itself, and not an a priori structure.

Nietzsche's understanding of bad conscience, Althusser's subject of interpellation, the unhappy consciousness in Hegel, and Freud's melancholia are all articulations of the subject that begin with a tropological turn, a move from the appropriation or incorporation of the outside into the self. But the condition of possibility for this change in the meaning of desire is always a sacrifice of the desiring body. I should clarify at the outset, although I will engage with this idea in depth later, that the subject, for Butler, is not only a matter of subjection to the Law (the subjected subject); the subject instead names a paradoxical space within which this reflexive turn of submission leads to a form of agency. The paradox is that the advent of this agency is not prior to subjection; instead, the two processes happen at the same time.

Bad conscience in Nietzsche is nothing other than a will to power that cannot affirm itself outside the organism. Because of the prohibitions imposed by the outside world, this will to power cannot continue in its original direction, and so it "decides" to discharge itself within the self. In *The Genealogy of Morals*, guilt is a "debt" occasioned by a damage that could not be repaired. Punishment is, on the contrary, a payment of this debt. Note that there is an economy of creditors and debtors here. In the last instance, isn't this how justice is understood in the West? Isn't this justice the unfolding of an economy of punishment and also (with scandalous concreteness) a monetary payment defined as redress, or repair for damage? Isn't this what the image of justice as a scale represents for us? Two stones on one side and one on the other: Doesn't this economy of punishment continue the Mosaic *lex talionis* or law of retaliation? This is the genealogy of morals that Nietzsche recounts.

For now I will set aside the problem of a "just economy" in order to return to it later. First, however, I want to underscore the obscenity of punishment, of this genealogy of retribution which leads to imprisonment when, according to what Derrida would call an incalculable calculus, there is no monetary sum that can compensate for the damage caused to another member of the community. And yes, the imprisonment of the body continues the economy of punishment of the Middle Ages. In *Discipline and Punish*, Foucault recounts how the prison led to an easing in punishment by torture, but this easing was only an *Aufhebung*, a sublation, since it is still the body that is the object of punishment and the commodity in the exchange. In prison, the body is the support of punishment. Although the state no longer lays claim to a limb [*miembro*] as a way of "charging" the condemned for his transgression, since this state is an institutionalized law, it clearly deprives the community of one member [*miembro*]: the offender. There is also, of course, the enormous problem of "crimes against humanity" for which no "commensurable" punishment can be found, so that the only recourse is pardon or forgiveness.

The subject is inaugurated, Butler says, when it turns against its own desire, that is, when it becomes capable of reproaching itself. This self-punishment reveals both forms of subordination: On the one hand, the internalization of external norms shows that the subject is now exercising its agency to subordinate itself; on the other hand, this same process shows that it has been subordinated by social power, compelled to recognize these norms as imperatives. The subject is therefore the site where a paradox is staged: The subject-as-agent is also the subject-as-subjected. The subject is subordinated to the law imposed from without; repressing its own desire, the subject subordinates itself. But what is behind this desire for a subjection that comes from two directions? The fear of death and the organism's desire to remain alive. One of the most apt and revelatory of Butler's arguments in *The Psychic Life of Power* has to do with the biological origins of the human being's desire for subjection. In this text, Butler connects subjection and self-subjection to the premature, vulnerable, and helpless state in which the human being is born. The newborn's dependency on an adult other who cares for it is translated into a promise: The other offers to sustain the organism, to keep it alive. The persistence of this affective tie is rooted in the fact that the fulfillment of this promise is conditioned on the small organism's subjection to the Law of the Other. Attachment is shot through with subordination. However, the organism also subordinates itself and represses its own desire to the same end: in order to survive. "'I would rather exist in subordination than not exist' is one formulation of this predicament (where the risk of 'death' is also possible)" (Butler, *Psychic Life* 7).[6] The subject is therefore the site of a paradoxical coexistence of heteronomy and autonomy. But there is another paradox or rather another aporia involved in the claim that the subject turns against itself, because the subject is the effect of this very turn. Inasmuch as the subject is the effect of a tropological turn, an internalization of the outside in the form of identifications, there is no subject, strictly speaking, that makes this turn, that is, the reflexive turn that inaugurates the subject. To underscore another one of Butler's key claims: The subject is also the denial or negation of its subordination and dependency. The subject is not aware of its perverse attachment to authority, and emerges in and through its denial of this subordination. For Butler, "[i]t is important to distinguish between the notion of the psyche, which includes the notion of the unconscious, and that of the subject, whose formation is conditioned by the exclusion of the unconscious" (206n4). Psyche and subject are thus notions that refer to different psychic functions. The subject is attachment in dependency and at the same time denial of this subordination. That is, the subject is also the agency that seeks to de-subordinate itself and that in this way demonstrates its subjection. Drawing on psychoanalysis, we can think of all the failures of repression as attempts at, and small successes with, rebellion: slips of the tongue, dreams, and symptoms, disavowed unconscious material that irrupts within consciousness, and, of course, all forms of eroticism. All of these forms of psychic functioning attest to the subject's desire for self-disintegration.

We could say that Butler's genealogy of the subject in *The Psychic Life of Power* is an ontogenetic profile that corresponds to the phylogenetic myth or myth of community that Freud recounts in *Totem and Taboo*. Civilization, which I propose to understand as a matter of radical responsibility for otherness, is paradoxically founded and sustained by the compulsive denial of a sacrifice, of a crime, or of a history of crime. History is founded on the awareness of guilt over parricide and, Freud seems to imply, on the secret of this crime. The parricidal horde's guilt was so great that the following generations were not openly told about its having murdered the father. But that some transgenerational communication took place and still takes place is, for Freud, undeniable. It is admittedly mysterious, however, that Freud does not venture to say, either in *Totem and Taboo* or in *Moses and Monotheism*, how or through what medium this phylogenetic memory was and is transmitted.

Everything begins with sacrifice, and the origin is always a crime. The ego, more precisely, is a guilty ego. There is no ego without crime, because the ego is the incorporation of guilt and therefore of the transgression itself. Before I am responsible, I am guilty, because one can only be radically responsible for a fault; I am only responsible for a violence that I have wielded. In order to be responsible, I have to first be a debtor. Every time that we say "I," we say in effect, "I, who am guilty . . ." The ego or "I," defined as the subject of a grammatical sentence, is one who responds in that it is compromised by an ontogenetic and phylogenetic transgression. The Althusserian subject of interpellation, which comes into being with a turn, when it responds to the call of authority, turns because it is guilty, a priori. This subject is a debtor, is in debt, from the beginning.

What does it owe? And to whom? What do we mean when we refer to owing or obligation [*el deber*], to our debts and duties, to what ought to be [*el deber ser*], to what you owe, to what I owe, to what we owe, to what they owe?

Debt and duty are imperatives that respond to an economy of sacrifice, as Derrida names it in *The Gift of Death*. "One does what one has to or what is owed [*Se hace lo que se debe*]" means that doing, that is, moral action, is the payment of a debt. In the beginning, we are all guilty of a crime, one that we have all always already committed. Butler says that our unconscious is the effect of the displacement of subordination. This does not mean that the content of the unconscious is limited to the denial of dependency; it means that the psyche's stratification, or in other words the fact that the psyche is an economy involving several different topological registers or layers, is the effect of a reflexive turn that does not encompass all the drives. The drives, the instincts, much of the desiring body is irrepressible. The repressed is paradoxically irrepressible. The repressed is only secret. The myth of sacrifice that Freud recounts in *Totem and Taboo* is phylogenetically passed on (again, Freud does not say exactly how) as a secret. Our unconscious is this inheritance, and it is also the "dirty little secret" or rather the big primitive secret that all we carry within us. This means that just as the singular unconscious is impossible to suffocate and can only be veiled, denied, negated, or repressed within the personal history of each of us, the "savagery" of the community is also invisible. If we follow the hypothesis that guides

Freud's social psychology, then every law, every institution, every nation-state, every community, and every religion is nothing other than the resistance required to repress this incestuous and cannibalistic savagery. And just as neurotic repression is not once and done, and just as the resistance that seeks to keep the repressed removed from consciousness requires a constant expenditure of energy, so too does civilization in all of its forms begin with the prohibition or at least the regulation of endogenous instincts, of cannibalistic and incestuous desires. This is precisely what accounts for civilization's constant "discontent."

Isn't this also precisely what Derrida means when he says that history is the history of responsibility or that history should be thought of as responsibility (*The Gift of Death* 4)? This history responds to the following questions: Why do these scenes repeat themselves? Why can an assassination, a sacrifice, not be once and done? Why Holocausts in the plural? Why is the history of the West a history of murders? Is it that the West has or is a melancholic economy, and that, as in melancholy, we only ever leave this state in order to enter a state of mania without having mourned the loss? And does the loss then return to haunt us? Does the shadow of the object then fall over the collective ego? At this point, we must remember that repression is not a psychic mechanism whose activation is once and done. The force of resistance that sometimes emerges victorious thus occasionally lets us act as subjects or as a community.[7] Moreover, as Freud explains in *Beyond the Pleasure Principle*, the death drive, or the drive to aggression or destruction, can be regulated but not overcome. Can it be, then, that in order to leave this melancholic repetition behind, we need to mourn all of the losses of which we are always already guilty? The difference between mourning and melancholia is a matter of two different economies. The work of mourning allows for an inversion of libido. After a tract of time — time is the only thing that can cure the loss, Freud seems to say in "Mourning and Melancholia" — investment in the lost object can give way to investment in another object or other objects. This, then, is a change of libidinal investments and is what the melancholic is incapable of achieving. The melancholic cannot be flexible or alter his or her libidinal economy and so ends up identifying with the lost object. The burden imposed thus follows from a turning against the self. I cite some of the most famous sentences from "Mourning and Melancholia":

> Thus the shadow of the object fell upon the ego, and the latter could henceforth be judged by a special agency, as though it were an object, the forsaken object. In this way an object-loss was transformed into an ego-loss and the conflict between the ego and the loved person into a cleavage between the critical activity of the ego and the ego as altered by identification. (SE 14: 249)

This means that the melancholic sacrifices himself or herself. The melancholic puts his or her ego to death in a sort of ritual sacrifice commemorating the lost loved one. "If you die, I'll die," or "I'd die for you" are therefore not, for the melancholic, merely dramatic phrases. They are promises to be fulfilled. The melancholic dwells in affective ambivalence. He or she suffers disproportionately from a loss and stages a drama. As we say in Mexico, the melancholic is a *teatrero*, a drama queen, who has neither discretion nor shame but openly expresses pain, showing and communicating it to everyone around. The excessive love and suffering caused by the loss originate, Freud says, in a place where the opposite feeling, hate, even led the melancholic to desire the loved one's death. The melancholic feels guilty for the death of the object. But Freud argues that, if we listen carefully, we can hear that the melancholic's complaints and reproaches are addressed to the lost object itself. The melancholic shares at least two things with the "primitive" in *Totem and Taboo*: First, he or she believes in the omnipotence of his or her desires and thoughts. That is, the melancholic believes that these caused the death of the object. And, second, his or her reproaches are always and for this reason moral in nature. The melancholic sees himself or herself as deplorable for having desired the death of the loved object. He or she shares with the member of Freud's primitive horde the sense of guilt for having annihilated this beloved being, though only at the level of desire, fantasy, and thought.

Thus our societies are melancholically structured. Because, in my view, we have not been able to resolve our primordial loss through mourning, our social, juridical, economic, and political systems are structured and organized in ways that make identification with the guilty ego a priori. This is a matter of brotherhoods—indeed, brotherhoods and not sisterhoods—that impose subject positions, offering options that are few and phallocentric. Only brothers who are male, strong, white, rich, and powerful are fully recognized by the law. All others have limited rights. No, we are not all equal before the law, because the law has excluded us in advance.[8] Butler's argument, however, is more complex. The community, the state in general, or the social order is melancholic because it cannot mourn its losses. And this is even more dramatic: The loss, says Butler, has not even been registered. We are therefore dealing not with a loss that has been repressed, but one that has been foreclosed. The structure of melancholy is one that excludes, on the basis of a loss. The melancholic subject is one who is structured by the radical exclusion of negativity: of the Black, the Indian, the feminine, the weak, the homosexual, the sex worker, the addict, and so forth. This subject is not merely one that denies its constitutive negativity, but one that sacrifices it. But we should not forget that the subject is the effect of the incorporation of the law. It is therefore the law "incarnated" in the text of the constitution and the "body" of all institutions that are structured melancholically and that give birth to subjects that are subjected both physically and morally. Modern states are repetitions of the totemic organization. They are phallocentric fraternities that, in order to sustain themselves, must displace all that they have desired and all that they were: They desired women and were weak, helpless. These figures, women and the weak, have been foreclosed as objects, and precisely for this reason they must be excluded and compulsively sought. Every institution is the staging of an originary exclusion. And despite all of these efforts, the excluded becomes the repressed unconscious, which produces effects.

Where do we go from here? First, we confront a discursive trap. If the subject is the incorporation of this system, then how can we escape it? In other words, how can we leave behind a structure that constitutes us structurally? The space in which we might turn away from the melancholic circuit—also the circuit of sacrifice—can be found paradoxically within the psyche, defined as what does not let itself be fully subjected, because it includes a drive that is always pulsating, that is insuperable and impossible to asphyxiate. The unconscious is thus a revolutionary force. But just as there is an economy that calculates and regulates "how much is enough" in psychic and social life, so there are revolutions and revolutions. We need to devise communities that can help us guide or give shape to the pulsating force of the drives, leading us toward the production of organizations that are ever more complex rather than ever simpler and more unified. (Unification implies the exclusion or annihilation of difference by the dominant. Or at least, no less undesirably, it implies a mode of inclusion that erases difference, that is, not an incorporation of difference but an assimilation.)

If one way of escaping the melancholic circuit involves entering another circuit that leads us toward death but at the same time toward the simple, identical, and undifferentiated, Butler argues that the itinerary of the social should allow for cuts in the path of the work of mourning, detours that make it possible for us to take other paths that are not circular, not circuits. Circuits always lead us back to the same places, but rivers, for instance, have many deltas. Mourning is in this sense an economy not of sacrifice but of Eros.[9] Within psychoanalytic theory, on the one hand, the possibility of mourning depends on the plasticity of the libido, that is, on the possibility that an investment in one object might be dispensed with in favor of another. This is, Freud says, not necessarily another subject; it could be a task, a project, an institution. The important thing in this economic transaction is that the investment involves an expenditure of energy, a form of work. On the other hand, however, sublimation is the only destiny for the drives that allows them to fulfill the desire for an object, where this object is not the original object of desire. Sublimation is not, like all of the other mechanisms of defense,[10] a matter of partial satisfaction. For psychoanalysis, artistic production is the paradigm of sublimation. Art encompasses—without rendering axiomatic, articulating, or conceptualizing—mystery, secrecy, loss, finitude, and absence, which are shown to be hidden. Art points to the path along which communities will need to travel in order to build societies that are ever more complex and ever more peaceful. Is this not what Freud suggests in a moving line from near the end of his letter to Einstein: "[W]hatever fosters the growth of civilization works at the same time against war"? (SE 22: 215).

Instinct, the drive, and desire are insuperable and inextinguishable forces that can only be subdued or calmed momentarily. As soon as they find a path that leads toward their satisfaction, they take it. The question is thus: How to go beyond this limit, how to build less cruel societies in which sacrifice would not need to be so bloody? To be sure, this would be a matter of another kind of economic regulation, one that recognizes the limit but does not translate the impossibility of fully overcoming violence and cruelty into a politics of resignation. Instead, this impossibility can be translated into an imperative, an eternal struggle and interminable project. It is true that the only space we have is a certain "economized" politics of violence. Perhaps the most romantic figure would be the figure of deferring violence, as one defers payment, saving it for later, and later . . .

It would thus be necessary to think of "communities of duelists [*duelistas*, also 'mourners'],"[11] communities of fighters who resist sovereign power, but who do so not with weapons, not with bloodshed, and not with lethal injections. Such injections are not matters of combat; rather, they annihilate and disappear the enemy. They do not involve the enemy in a fight, a confrontation, or a duel. By contrast, duelists would have two fundamental tasks: first, not to give up, not to desist in the battle against death's squadrons, and second not to let their libido become fixed in absolute representations, because although living with others surely, inherently involves some renunciations, losses and sacrifices, "some" here means that these are politically chosen. Duelists mourn the dead or those who have been negated, and they manage to re-invest libido erotically, productively, and creatively after the loss of their loved objects. Duelists are not melancholics or suicidal; nor do they sacrifice themselves for the other who has died or been lost. Instead, if necessary, they fight for this other. They are not so many Bartlebys[12] because they respond, move, and act. Bartleby with his refusals does not respond and does not offer a model of action or political resistance, because he does not make demands, does not denounce, and, in the most general terms, does not provoke the other (in this case, his boss) to change his subjective position or his relation to power. The master in this story changes his address and finds new subordinates to oppress, but he does not cease to oppress.

It is the social contract of shared responsibility that Bartleby the scrivener breaks. And shared responsibility implies not only complicity in crime, but also being subjected to the same yoke, interpellated by the same authority. Bartleby seems not to have engaged in this transaction, and for this reason he does not respond. He even calls his own status as a living being into question. Is he alive? Derrida might say that he is a zombie, an undecidable, because he gazes at his interrogator without recognizing the latter's almost natural right to be addressed. At the same time, this gaze that does not linger also casts doubt on the interlocutor's (or reader's) life, since Bartleby's non-response makes him doubt his own existence. Am I alive or am I a ghost who bears witness? Bartleby's resistance to action results in an act of disregard, a misrecognition of the one who interpellates him, who calls and who therefore must be spoken to, confessed to, lied to, complained to, solicited, or in any case answered. The scrivener's refusal could be interpreted as a way of obtaining a certain sovereignty. But the latter is in fact strictly delimited, since the narrator insists that Bartleby surrenders to death, and in his resistance he does not reach out to anyone. (We should not forget that while he occupies the offices, he is alone.) Bartleby is an egoist who does nothing to effect a change in anyone's political or psychic circumstances. Bartleby's response, which is a non-response, thus breaks with, jeopardizes, and sacrifices humanity's first social contract, the one that, according to Freud, is fundamental and foundational: shared responsibility.

3

Beyond the Limit of the Death Drive

Eros

Life and Death Drives

Freud writes in *Beyond the Pleasure Principle* that the death drive never operates on its own and is always accompanied by Eros. It is silent but not solitary. After the Freudian discovery of the insuperable and unbeatable death drive—that is, after Freud's presentation of this drive as inherent not only in human nature, but in nature more generally—the question that looms for any pacifist or lover of ecology[1] in all its forms is this one: Must we surrender to this idea without complaints, without resistance? Must we submit? Should we give up our weapons since, in fact, we do not have weapons capable of countering the forces of death and destruction? The response to each of these questions is a resounding "no." But at the same time, this response cannot be a simple no. We need to find a theoretical foundation to sustain the possibility of going beyond the death drive. And we must do this not in the interest of a learned theoretical enterprise, but rather, more urgently, in order to arm ourselves with weapons of other kinds, in order to build these and find new uses for them as we seek to establish that this is both possible and right. This is also an effort to convince—through discursive seduction, but also by means of political conquest, where "conquest" is again defined as seduction and not colonization—more and more of our "friends" of the need to join us in the formation of a battalion that I would like to call erotic. The horizon of this battalion's march is the coming into being of friendship. As Marcuse writes:

> Does Eros, in spite of all the evidence, in the last analysis work in the service of the death instinct, and is life really only one long "detour to death"? But the evidence is strong enough, and the detour is long enough to warrant the opposite assumption. Eros is defined as the great unifying force that preserves all life. The ultimate relation between Eros and Thanatos remains obscure. (*Eros and Civilization* 26–27)

I begin this chapter by evoking friendship because I am thinking against the backdrop of the last chapter of Derrida's *Politics of Friendship*, and especially its last words: "O my democratic friends . . ." (306). In this text, Derrida calls on his "democratic friends" to show that democracy is founded on a certain form of equality: equality among siblings or brothers, where brotherhood is defined as one of the highest forms of friendship. (The sibling relationship privileged in republics is brotherhood and not sisterhood.) It is not the main goal of this chapter to address the problem of phallocentrism in or as the politics of friendship, but I would like to pause to consider, rather than avoid, some urgent questions that must be addressed in the analysis of politics generally and Western democratic politics in particular. Women are not only excluded from the everyday functioning of this politics; their exclusion is at the beginning of this politics as such, which, as we know, is a system designed for and by men, one that makes room for men's bodies only. To be clear, I am not saying only that we, as women, should be able to enter and take part in politics — which is obviously true — but rather that we cannot enter as women, with these bodies, because political discourse at every level, from the deepest to the most superficial, is responsive to others, to bodies that do and desire other things, bodies with specific biological characteristics and with different capacities, perceived to be less vulnerable. Here I set aside this detour in order to return to it with the critical attention and dedication it deserves in another context.

I am arguing that we must look for ways to account theoretically for the possibility of realizing or bringing into being more erotic, more peaceful, more just, and more democratic forms of social organization. When I say "more democratic," I am thinking not only equality defined in terms of political or civil rights, but also — in equal or greater measure and all the more urgently in so-called Third World countries — equality in economic and social terms. I have just said, "in equal or greater measure," and it seems to me that one necessary condition of being politically free is the meeting of economic and social needs — including not only those needs that are basic, as we hear in the demagogic discourses of all Third World politicians, but also those that are specific. Derrida writes: "When will we be ready for an experience of freedom and equality that is capable of respectfully experiencing that friendship, which would at last be just, just beyond the law and measured up against its measurelessness?" (306). Note that, for Derrida, freedom and equality are two experiences that are distinct, but they are inescapably related, or must be if we want to open the space for democracy and friendship. In other words, democracy is not a mandate or a form of government, but rather a space that friendship requires, that is, the necessary condition for equality and freedom. Perhaps something like a perfect dose of both liberalism and communism is indispensable here. Likewise, we should not ignore the fact that Derrida thinks of friendship as the experience of a justice that exceeds law and rights, because whereas law is the formulation of the universal, justice is only and radically a singular phenomenon. This does not mean that friendship is a matter of singular relations, but rather that it responds to unrepeatable situations that cannot be measured by any law, and that it therefore must be a practice, something done, something understood and interpreted according to the logic of what is "each time unique."[2]

We can locate some theoretical foundations to sustain the possibility of a pacifist and erotic political project at the heart of Freud's own work. That is, we do not need to go beyond Freud in order to go beyond the death drive. Neither do we need to go beyond Freud in order to overcome his pessimism. Freud himself, on more than one occasion (though not on many more), claimed to be an optimist, or at least, if that sounds exaggerated, implied that under certain political and social circumstances we might think of another, better world.

Although after the Holocaust or other genocides, it may be impossible and even foolish to insist that there could be a legal model capable of guiding humanity toward "perpetual peace," we cannot and must not stop remembering the importance of at least working toward, or dying in the pursuit of, such peace, which also means resisting radical evil. As Judith Butler writes: "Many people say that arguing for nonviolence is unrealistic, but perhaps they are too enamored of reality. When I ask them whether they would want to live in a world in which no one was arguing for nonviolence, where no one held out for that impossibility, they always say no" (*The Force of Nonviolence* 64).

Let us begin by analyzing the irruption of the life drive within the psyche, an irruption that interrupts the autonomous functioning of the death drive. It follows from Freud's interpretation of culture as a source of discontent that, for Freud, there is a limit to the political transformation of society, guided by the ideal of democratic inclusion. This limit is the death drive or the destructive drive, in that this is a tendency that is insuperable and inherent in human existence. Nevertheless, in *Beyond the Pleasure Principal*, human nature is ambivalent. Even while it is destructive and antisocial, it is erotic and based in coexistence. In this regard, Freud and Kant share a premise. For Kant, human nature is not pacifist; peace is the product of conscious will, a victory won by conscience. Still, this conscience and its cultural achievements emerge from human nature, and this is ambivalent for Kant as well. In *To Perpetual Peace*, Kant argues that human beings are naturally predisposed to evil in a way that makes them antisocial, that causes them to act immorally and pursue evil ends. But at the same time they are endowed (by God) with reason, and this is what motivates the quest for perpetual peace:

> . . . there is in man a still greater, though presently dormant, moral aptitude to master the evil principle in himself (a principle he cannot deny) and to hope that others will also overcome it. For otherwise the word *right* would never leave the mouths of those nations that want to make war on one another, unless it were mockingly, as when the Gallic prince declared, "Nature has given the strong the prerogative of making the weak obey them." (356)

From this perspective, we should think of human existence as engaged in a rebellious revolt, or as in the midst of a neurotic battle, between the life drives and the destructive drives, or, following Kant, between what we could call a natural predisposition to evil and the pacifist aspirations of rational conscience.

In "Formulations on the Two Principles of Psychic Functioning" and in *Beyond the Pleasure Principle*, Freud posits a primal state of rest, but one that is very quickly disrupted by the imperious demands arising from the organism's internal needs. The paradoxical movement of the two great psychic tendencies, driven by Eros and Thanatos, can be seen from the beginning of human life. On the one hand, the pleasure principle appears, tending toward the total discharge of tension and thus identified with a deathly impulse; on the other hand, we find the reality principle, which adapts to the limitations and benefits of external reality and responds to the survival instinct, or what Freud elsewhere calls "*the exigencies of life*" (SE 1: 297; emphasis in original).

Basic bodily necessities are thus experienced as urgently in need of satisfaction. These are what lead to the modification of the psychic apparatus's primal tendency to avoid all stimulation and return immediately to an inorganic state, as Freud describes it in *Beyond the Pleasure Principle*: a return that is a circuitous path to death. This modification consists in the creation of a reserve of energy (stimulation, later libido) that keeps the organism alive in its search for an internal alteration that might alleviate its sense of bodily need. Freud calls this paradigmatic experience an "experience of satisfaction" (SE 18: 42). Crucially, here the reserve of energy is nothing other than a mnemic trace. However, it is not only fundamental biological needs that the organism strives to satisfy; according to Freud's descriptions of the "origin of the psyche" (and indeed the origin of life, to which I will return later), the organism also tends to ward off the stimulation that comes from the external world. We could thus say, on the one hand, that every organism experiences internal or external stimulation as an affront, and, on the other hand, that life is set in motion in order to ward off this stimulation. Here I will pause to consider in more detail Freud's descriptions of some psychic mechanisms dedicated to "living life out."

The Freudian psychic apparatus is an artifact whose mechanisms are set in motion in the encounter between the one and the other. This psychic apparatus results from the violent confrontation between two forces that encounter one another, where both seek to affirm themselves. Here, for Freud, the one resists the irruption of the other and seeks to avoid the excitation that the other provokes. The origin of the psyche is the organic body's need (Ἀνάγκη) to ward off its own alteration by the external world. All psychic mechanisms work toward this end, and this, Freud claims, results in the ruling principle of psychic life, which he calls the pleasure principle.

Paradoxically if not contradictorily, the pleasure principle ends up merging with the death drive, since it works toward the diminution of tension that, reaching zero, necessarily implies the organism's death.[3] In order to resolve this dilemma, Freud introduces the principle of constancy, which seeks to maintain a minimum of tension in the organization in order to avoid total discharge. Still, this constancy does not operate according to a linear or chronological temporality. Instead, Freud insists, it operates according to "a vacillating rhythm":

> It is as though the life of the organism moved with a vacillating rhythm. One group of drives rushes forward to reach the final aim of life as swiftly as possible; but when a particular stage in the advance

> has been reached, the other group jerks back to a certain point to make a fresh start and so prolong the journey. (SE 18: 41)

But what forms the basis of all of this speculation, as Freud himself calls it?[4] An interpretation of life and even of the origin of life. For Freud, life is fundamentally made up of two tendencies: tension and the return to the discharge of this tension — not a direct return, but rather a circuitous one, a circuit that departs from and leads to the same place by way of a detour. Freud notes: "The attributes of life were at some time evoked in inanimate matter by the action of a force of whose nature we can form no conception" (SE 18: 38). The obvious question that inevitably jumps out at us at this point in Freud's interpretation has to do with the duration of life: Why does the process that he describes take time? And what forces or interests determine the organism's detour or circuitous route to death? In other words, why is death not simply a short-circuit? To formulate this question is effectively to ask: Why does the psyche exist? Indeed, in Freud's interpretation of the psyche and of life in *Beyond the Pleasure Principle*, the psychic apparatus turns out to be a machine that mediates between the organism's life and its death. The psyche is a space of deferral that is opened up by a phenomenon that is neither pure life nor pure death. We could thus say that we are dealing with a machine of *life death*, as Derrida thinks of the parenthesis between the beginning of life and death, where these are not two different phenomena, but rather part of one economy.[5] But this does not mean that life's duration is only deathly or suicidal. Life is a constant psychic tension that involves both discharge and recharging. (This is the economy of desire, which I will not address in this text but should be kept in mind.) Life can be understood as a radical affirmation when it leads toward action with the aim of discharging tension by any means possible. Yet to say that life, in this sense, leads toward death does not mean that it *is* death. As I noted earlier, for Derrida, life and death should be thought of as the same phenomenon. We are dealing, then, with an economy of sameness and not one of identity, because identity has no economy but is rather the paralysis of substance, ultimate, autonomous, and unalterable. We must remember that the relation between life, the psyche, and death is speculative in every sense of the word: in the sense of an economy that can only calculate results, that is, an economy without certainty, but also in the sense of a mirror reflection in which all identities, origins, or unities are lost, because they do not exist. And they do not exist because at the "origin" of what we might call every singularity there is another, the mark or imprint of the other. Thus, in every psychic phenomenon — dreams, slips of the tongue, desires, fantasies, thoughts, and so on — life and death are the speculative doubles of one another.

The principle of constancy that Freud introduces into his discourse in *Beyond the Pleasure Principle* sustains life through the formation of a reserve of energy whose total discharge is always deferred. In other words, the principle of constancy defers the death drive. All of the psychic apparatus's functions thus attest to a certain saving or storage of energy (desires that are long-held, desires that are unfulfilled or unfulfillable) that in Freudian terms corresponds to memory.

Memory is what is kept or guarded in the form of postponed pleasure. It is also the path by which tensions will be discharged in the future. This sort of archive constitutes a protection against death. Freud explains in the *Project* how the psychic apparatus reserves a certain quantity of excitation as a defense against self-exterminating discharge. In this sense, the death drive is, on one hand, what leads to the necessity of creating this reserve and, on the other hand and at the same time, what leads us to destroy every trace in the Derridean sense. In other words, the archive is made possible by the death drive, that is, by an originary drive to destruction that facilitates the archive's genesis. Life is the psyche; the psyche is memory. Let us therefore deduce, as in a *modus ponens*, that life is memory. The psyche mediates between life and death. Another simple deduction, another *modus ponens*, thus follows: This mediation is memory defined as a reserve. For Freud, as for Derrida, this psychic mediation is writing. Already in the neurological model of the psychic apparatus in the *Project*, the psyche is shaped by writing.[6] As I explained in Chapter 1, the process that Freud names facilitation, pathbreaking, or the opening of a passage (*Bahnung*) is a writing of traces through which stimulation is discharged. The stimulus comes into contact with the organization's resistance (or the protection against stimuli) and opens a channel for the discharge of energy that then leads to memory. The organization's resistance to alteration by means of a force of rejection is precisely what causes the stimulus to produce an inscription. Memory is therefore the archive of the organism's alterations, but we should not forget that these modifications correspond to traces that are themselves marks or channels for discharge. Nor should we forget the other fundamental aspect of the phenomenon of facilitation or *Bahnung*: that this opening of a passage changes with each repetition, becoming ever more passable. Let us recall briefly Freud's description in the *Project* of the two (later three) different types of neurons that correspond to the two fundamental (and mutually exclusive) functions of the psychic apparatus, perception and memory, associated with ϕ and ψ neurons, respectively. These two types of neurons are differentiated not structurally, but rather exclusively in quantitative terms, that is, in the quantity of resistance that their "contact-barriers" offer to the passage of energy. ψ neurons are associated with memory in that they forcefully resist stimulation and are altered, becoming writing, in and through their encounters with stimuli. But, interestingly, with each recurrence of such an encounter, the paths that these neurons create become ever more passable, to the point that, Freud says, ψ neurons become ϕ neurons.[7] This means that the psyche as mnemic machine is led inevitably and inherently toward death defined as a weakening of the resistance that defers discharge. The resistance of the contact-barriers thus fulfills two functions that must not be thought of as contradictory: It retains and dissipates, disappears, or disperses. Psychic life (and life in general, according to Freud's mythology, to which I will soon return) emerges in and through the resistance to stimuli that gives rise to writing, that is, to a phenomenon of mnemic archiving that gives rise to a sort of erotic detour before death. Let us again recall that the route to death—that is, life—can be erotic or deathly, can be guided by Eros or Thanatos depending on the singularity of each psychic economy. Thus the paradoxical phenomenon of *life death* belongs to the economy of writing.

Recall Socrates in Plato's *Phaedrus*, where writing is defined as a pharmakon, a poison. Here, again, Socrates calls writing a bastard discourse whose meaning no one can defend because it has been abandoned by its "father," left to its fate. Socrates explains, citing the Egyptian king Thamus, that writing only makes men more forgetful, because they cease to use their memories. Yet Derrida indicates that the pharmakon is not only a poison; it also functions as a medicine. I would underscore the "med-," the medium or mediation, in medicine: writing operates between the extremes that correspond to the beginning and the end of life. It is a parenthesis, a detour, impasse, or circuitous route to death.

We should note that, like every medicine or remedy, writing is at once a means to an end and is itself a means or mediation within space-time.[8] In psychic terms, writing is shown to be not a poison that is lethal for memory, but rather memory itself (and we should not forget that memory will self-destruct when the resistance offered by the ψ neurons is weakened, and the paths left open by these neurons become fully open, that is, when these neurons become ϕ neurons). Psychic writing, or the psyche as writing, is a medium or site of mediation, and like all mediation it consists of a negotiation between extremes that, within mental space, turn out to be the extremes of life and death. But in addition, the psyche as writing or mediation operates through mechanisms that activate the economy of life and death. The psyche is therefore an artifact whose technique is writing, defined as a mediation between a beginning and an insuperable end. This writing is mnemic, because it is nothing other than the tracing of furrows through which tension (life) is discharged. Memory is merely the opening of passages in which life is lived out. I would underscore the passive voice here, because the "living out" is not immediate.

Freud is right to call the psyche an "apparatus." Given all of the above, we might wonder what type of apparatus it is, and we might respond that the psychic apparatus is a "bio-artifact." It is a "bio-artifact" first because it is a machine for mediating between a living organism and the world, and second because it is an equation that involves the material body and the other. The "equation" here is a matter not of subtraction but of something left over, a remainder in the Derridean sense. Though singular, the remainder is not indivisible. It is a singularity shot through with and haunted by the other. For several reasons, the relationship between the world and this bio-artifact is specular. As I noted earlier, here the one and the other mirror one another, producing a specular image or infinite reflection. They are two different, differentiated things, but this is a matter not of identity but of sameness. The bio-artifact is the product of an economic negotiation between the one and the other, between a body and the world. This economy is also speculative, because it is never stabilized and because its ultimate objective is not an investment, in the sense in which Freud refers to libidinal investment in objects or representations, but rather the deferral of death. The psychic apparatus, defined as a machine for economic mediation, also incorporates the economy of the outside (understood in terms of biopolitics, as in the work of Foucault or Butler, among others). But there is a breaking point; that is, incorporation never arrives at the totality of the one. There is something that resists otherness and remains. But this remainder cannot be thought of as unmodifiable, static, and always stable. The remainder is not a substance, but rather an agent of change—an agent in the sense that it completes actions, only never from a position of purity, but instead from a place of contamination and communication, heteronomous and heterogeneous. What remains is alterable; it moves and changes shape, and its exchange value also changes. What resists is thus also the product of a negotiation between the one and the other. For as long as the organism lives, its relation to the other modifies its whole economy, and the remainder always changes its value or (geopolitical) location.

The psychic apparatus is, then, a bio-artifact that sets life in motion, but always in the form of a detour (or circuit) leading toward death. Freud assures us that in the beginning life was a disturbance: "[T]he life process of the individual leads for internal reasons to an abolition of chemical tensions, that is to say, to death, whereas union with the living substance of a different individual increases these tensions, introducing what may be described as fresh 'vital differences' which must then be lived off" (SE 18: 55). In this sense, the death drive would be the fundamental tendency in psychic life that at once activates the economy of the machine, the psychic apparatus, and leads it toward its own destruction.[9] The force that is behind the economy that governs both the "return to death" and the pressure of life—that is, the pressure that activates a certain resistance to and deferral of total discharge or short-circuiting—is "auto-tely,"[10] defined as a search for death or an ending proper to each organism. Auto-tely is nothing other than a delay or deferral of death. Death must be postponed for later, for that moment when death will be my own death. Within what we could call the logic of the repetition compulsion, as in all processes of writing, we thus find a wait, a state of expectation. The psychic apparatus's tendency toward repetition implies a process that pulls it toward a prior state, but where this return or restitution must necessarily involve waiting for a specific moment, the moment of "my own death." My death must be that which is my own; or, as Freud says, every organism seeks to die in "its own fashion."

Beyond auto-tely, Freud speculates that this vital detour is evolutionary in its origins. This means that living organisms have become more complex because they have been affected—and, I would add, altered—by external forces and other living organisms. The more complex they become, the more their lives are prolonged as the circuit that leads toward death becomes more complicated to traverse. Thus the path toward death corresponds to evolutionary history:

> For a long time, perhaps, living substance was thus being constantly created afresh and easily dying, till decisive external influences altered in such a way as to oblige the still surviving substance to diverge ever more widely from its original course of life and to

> make ever more complicated *détours* before reaching its aim of death. These circuitous paths to death, faithfully kept by the conservative drives, would thus present us today with the picture of the phenomena of life. (SE 18: 39; translation modified)

Beyond the errors and the interpretive violence in Freud's reading of Darwin—as when Freud suggests that evolution only leads to further complexity and is never simplifying in its effects—the important thing to note here is that the organism's life is more prolonged the more it is affected by other vital forces. Isn't this Eros? Eros is the force that tends toward the formation of ever more complex organizations, that is, the tendency to union, to addition and not the destruction or elimination of synthesis: "In this way the libido of our sexual drives would coincide with the Eros of the poets and philosophers which holds all living things together" (SE 18: 50; translation modified). Freud offers another speculation about this economy: The psyche and human existence are divided between the forces of Thanatos and those of Eros. But we should not forget that Eros is a tendency and thus not an organization; it is an infinite movement and not a substance. In this sense, erotic efforts are and must be tireless, because Eros is a horizon, always an open one. But in Freud's dystopian vision, when Eros seems to take the form of a "drive towards perfection," Freud adds that this impulse only "appears in a minority of human individuals" who seek to repress certain inherent, antisocial impulses (SE 18: 42; translation modified). Such an impulse is therefore not valid theoretically, but rather a consoling illusion. The life sciences have demonstrated that evolution is not progressive by nature, that for many organisms evolution is retrograde or that progress in one feature can come at the cost of an involution in another (SE 18: 36–37). In psychoanalysis, repression does not extinguish the drives, no force renounces its effort to affirm itself, and, since desire always renews itself, no sublimation suffices to bring about its cancellation. Like all other aspects of psychic life, the work of sublimation requires reiteration.

After the speculative chapter in *Beyond the Pleasure Principle*, Freud interrupts his philosophizing[11] and states that it is necessary to turn toward biology to establish with certainty that death is a natural law and thus that auto-tely has a scientific and not only a poetic or mythical foundation. But he immediately anticipates the conclusion of his recourse to experimental science: Biology has been, he notes, unable to define life. That is, there is no mathematical limit that separates life from death. "[T]he whole concept of death," Freud says, "melts away under [natural scientists'] hands" (SE 18: 45).

Freud then describes more than one experiment involving protozoa, noting that from these experiments scientists reached contradictory conclusions. Finally, in a very Freudian gesture, he discards all of the findings that contradict his speculations, although he does retain those offered by A. Weismann. This German biologist draws a distinction, in the living substance of multicellular organisms, between a mortal soma and other, "potentially immortal" germ cells. When the organism dies, the latter are capable of forming a new soma, a new body. He concludes that single-celled organisms are immortal because in them the individual organism and the germ cell are one and the same. Here his fundamental claim is that death is not a natural law of living substance, but affects only complex organisms, for whom it is an adaptive mechanism that responds to "the external conditions of life." For the soma already equipped with immortal germ cells, an unlimited, infinite life would be redundant and pointless. Freud says: "When this differentiation had been made in the multicellular organisms, death became possible and expedient" (SE 18: 46). On one hand, reproduction is therefore not an effect of death, but rather something proper to living matter; on the other hand, it is cellular reproduction that introduces mortality.

Relying on the work of Alexander W. von Goette, a German zoologist, Freud argues that death is a direct consequence of reproduction, which for Goette means sexual reproduction. This idea will guide Freud's conception of life death. At the end of Chapter VI in *Beyond the Pleasure Principle*, Eros is at the same time, undecidably, the force that ties all life together and the force that hyperbolically sends the organism hurtling toward an inanimate state.

In addition, at the end of *Beyond the Pleasure Principle*, the reproduction that takes place through the disturbance that is copulation, defined as the effect of an encounter between two organisms, contributes to an increase in the complexity of life, impelling the organism in its search for its own death. Eros is the force that drives the organism toward the world, forcing it out of its own Nirvana and obliging it to come into contact with otherness, that is, with the other who alters it. All the paraphernalia of reproduction—and all of the undeniable vicissitudes and inconveniences that this form of sexuality implies for living substance: the struggle for existence, the survival of the fittest, or, in more everyday words, flirtation, courtship, jealousy, and even crimes of passion—entail at the same time the need, or Ἀνάγκη, to return to a previous inanimate state, the effort to live life out. For internal reasons, Freud explains, the living tends toward the leveling of tension and then toward its total discharge. But during this process, curiously, the organism also seeks union with another living substance. This encounter leads to an elevation of tension, a tension that will have to be dislodged or discharged.

In addition to being conservative, the drives—whether of life or of death—would seem to be narcissistic. Eros seeks to reproduce itself, Thanatos to return to it simple, anemic unity. To be sure, scientific evidence, poetic evidence, philosophical speculation, and all good fiction reveal an undeniable tendency in life to seek its own destruction. Not only human beings, but also lions, dolphins, jacarandas, ants, beetles, and all other inhabitants of the immense kingdom of the living—that is, all living things—seem to be imperiously moved by the laws of the selfish gene and the suicidal gene. And yet something resists, another force. This erotic force—which complicates everything and perhaps only leads to impasse or to a circuitous path toward destruction and disintegration—is what sets a whole mechanism in motion, a complex organic and psychic technique for mediating between the beginning and the end. Life is guided, or at least has been guided until now, inevitably toward death. But the "in-between" that is Eros differs enormously from mere inertia. In any economy of the same, life and death, two phenomena that oppose each other, cannot be differentiated from one another in a clear and stable manner. An economy implies processes and techniques of mediation. The psyche is thus a bio-artifact, because it mediates the reflex arc or neural pathway between the two. The Freudian psychic apparatus is not a simple system for the discharge of stimuli; it is a machine of life death. All psychic mechanisms serve to defer death for later, and the psyche is thus an artifact that works to achieve delay. The psyche is, in this sense, a bio-artifact of the good life death.

Derrida says in "Freud and the Scene of Writing," without leaving any room for doubt, that the discovery of "delay" is Freud's ("Freud and the Scene of Writing," in *Writing and Difference* 203). Thus, according to Derrida, Freud's discovery is one that has to do with the temporality of the psychic apparatus. If the time of memory is one that leaves things for later, that irrupts at another moment, in a repetition that opens a future, then it is also a time that opens life up with a promise. What does it promise? I would like to speculate that it offers life a space for different and new possibilities. This is the time of a trace, an opening of paths through which tensions to come will be discharged, where the choice of one path over others leads to qualitative change. These furrows will then mediate discharge; that is, they *delay* discharge, because this is a matter of mediation and not of electric shock. This means that the more the psychic text is written and the more complex it is, the more death and destruction will be deferred for later.

In this time of delay, tomorrow becomes a place of possibility, because we cannot know with absolute certainty the destiny of what is deferred, saved for later. Or rather, there is no destiny; there is a future that we cannot know with absolute certainty. Isn't the temporality of delay thus characteristic of every machine? Isn't the machine, any machine, whether a virtual or a material one, a device that seeks to postpone the end, or finitude, our own and that of life in general? Isn't technology the science that seeks to prolong life, even if it is only a matter of a singular life, as in the case of machines meant for destruction? Even the use of machines meant for mass destruction always follows from a calculation according to which someone or something should die, life should be violently and cruelly interrupted, in order that someone or something else survive. Technology is the science of the economy of life death. Every machine is sustained by a calculation between the one and the other. This is what the machine or the machinic mediates. In other words, as it moves toward the insuperable end, within this temporality of delay, the machinic opens, in time, the space for infinite possibilities.

The machinic is the radicalization, the *mise en abyme*, of freedom. In "The Question concerning Technology," Heidegger argues that the essence of technology is not technical at all. The text opens with a gesture typical of Heidegger, a return to the Greeks:

> From earliest times until Plato the word *technē* is linked with the word *epistēmē*. Both words are names for knowing in the widest sense. They mean to be entirely at home in something, to understand and be expert in it. Such knowing provides an opening up. It reveals whatever does not bring itself forth and does not yet lie here before us, whatever can look and turn out now one way and now another. . . . Thus what is decisive in *technē* does not lie at all in making and manipulating nor in the use of means, but rather in the aforementioned revealing. It is as revealing, and not as manufacturing, that *technē* is a bringing-forth. ("The Question" 13)

Heidegger's forceful and radical critique in this text is not a critique of technology in general, but rather a critique of modern technology, which has forgotten its original meaning as an unveiling of the truth. Modern technology positions itself as means and a task for humanity. Moreover—and here is what is dangerous about it—modern technology has "challeng[ed]" and "set[] upon nature," turning it into a reserve of energy ("Question" 14, 15). This is, for Heidegger, the current definition of technology, one that corresponds to an instrumental, anthropological, and anthropocentric understanding.

Although the essence of technology is not technical at all, the danger of setting nature in place affects nature without radically altering it, that is, without encompassing it. It is important to underscore here that what technology reveals can be revealed in more ways than one. In other words, there is another possibility for technology, one that Heidegger finds recorded in Hölderlin's "Patmos": "*But where danger is, grows / The saving power also*" (qtd. in "Question" 42; emphasis in original). This means that the essence of technology harbors a power of salvation. The essence of technology is mysterious. It is not itself the danger; rather, its ethos can be guided toward a dangerous destiny, or not. The danger thus follows from Dasein's freedom to take one path or another, to realize one or another of technology's possibilities.

In psychic terms, we can say Eros and Thanatos are not identical just because they are driven toward the same end. The paths along which they arrive at death are different, incommensurable. There are narcissisms and narcissisms; there is more than one kind of Narcissus. Eros seeks out itself, to be sure, but it also seeks another and, in addition, life outside itself. Eros is like an altruistic gene. Freud notes that Weismann posits a difference between the mortal soma and the germ cells in living organisms; this difference coincides with his own dualist conception of the forces that govern life and that compel the organism to dwell in the middle, in a space of tension between life and death. Likewise, it is clear that, from this perspective, death cannot be thought of without sexual reproduction; it is also clear that the death drives are associated from the first with the life drives.

The psychic machine is flexible in this sense. It can produce more life or lead to annihilation. This mediation takes place through different trajectories, and we must not forget that these itineraries are mnemic paths traced in and through the encounter with the other's violence. Memory is the mark of the other, and of our resistance to this other. The other creates memory because it writes on the one; indeed, it writes the one, and this writing takes the form of paths cut into the one, paths through which tension will be discharged. In other words, memory, defined as psychic writing, gives rise to the differences in itineraries. These can be paths that lead to the destruction of the one and the other, or they can be paths along which to seek out organizations that are ever more complex.

The psyche and human existence form an open economy; that is, they are constituted in and through the tension between the forces of Thanatos and those of Eros. Proactive resistance must therefore be thought of as a force that can counter destructive tendencies, because Eros is a force that tends toward the formation of ever more complex organizations, that is, toward union, toward addition and not destruction or the elimination of processes of synthesis. Again, according to Freud, "the libido of our sexual drives would coincide with the Eros of the poets and philosophers which holds all living things together" (SE 18: 50; translation modified).

So we can assume that the effort to reconcile all differences is chimerical and that a certain tension is inescapable without thereby claiming that the death drive must simply be accepted, or that the passive acceptance of war is inevitable. Freud's view of this tension suggests instead that we need an ethics of vigilance, in which humanity would always remain attentive, opposing and denouncing any politics that incites violence or discrimination, or that relies on calls to hatred.

A close and careful reading of *Beyond the Pleasure Principle* makes clear that there is no principle, mechanism, or psychic function beyond the limit of the death drive, according to Freud. The seven chapters of Freud's text begin with an analysis of the possibility that there might be a theoretical successor to the pleasure principle, operating autonomously of it. And yet each of the book's sections concludes that there is in fact no definite route leading to this conclusion, that each of the tendencies that might seem to call the supremacy of the pleasure principle into question is no more than a simple detour around or inversion of it, that is, that these forces or mechanisms in fact operate in the service of the pleasure principle, like a sovereign's servants. The only thing left to us that might let us resist destruction and death, according to Freud's treatise, is Eros. But here Eros is not understood as a force that is completely distinct from Thanatos. Instead, Eros is a tendency that displaces and delays the drive to destruction. This is no small feat, but neither is it manna from heaven. In other words, it does not resolve the problem of the death drive once and for all, but rather represents a work in progress. Eros requires constant effort because it does not belong to the order of essence. Neither is it a substance that might be obtained through a kind of psychic alchemy, or a matter of a social contract capable of neutralizing the force of Thanatos. Eros belongs to an ontology of the gerundive, because it is a matter of the work of mediation. Erotic efforts interrupt the direct path to death or destruction, and although this path might lead imminently to an eschatological end, Eros manages to modify the journey to this end. We could therefore say that the path leading to death is a closed circle, but the erotic path is a complex detour. But I want to emphasize that the path of Eros is longer, that it implies mediation and interrupts the passage to inertia, which returns us to the more direct route to death immediately. I have already noted that the psyche is also a mediation, and that this delay of discharge fundamentally implies that, at least for a time, desire is fulfilled or deferred in the realm of the imaginary. For Freud, the fact that the drive can be satisfied in the psyche—that is, in the realms of the imaginary or the representational—results from the fact that it can take a regressive path. That is, the impulse to discharge, which is always directed toward motor action and is unleashed on the world, can be redirected toward a virtual object or postponed for a time, mediated by the psyche. Psychic space is erotic space. By this I do not mean that all psychic economies are erotic economies. I mean instead that, on the one hand, the creation of this space is an erotic possibility, and, on the other hand, that this is a path of defusion and sublimation.

The Regressions of the Psyche and Erotic Possibility

The Regressive Path to Psychic Discharge: The Dream as Paradigm

In *The Interpretation of Dreams*, Freud identifies two trajectories for psychic work. In states of wakefulness, the psyche generally follows the progressive path that leads from a perception of the drive to a motor extreme, as it seeks to discharge stimulation through action. The other path is regressive and is characteristic of the dreamwork, since it is precisely our access to motion that is deactivated while we sleep. In dreams, our internal impulses seek discharge through action, but they find this path closed and therefore "regress," causing excitations to our perceptual system. This is why, Freud explains, we watch a "film" or experience a "hallucination" during sleep.

In addition to being a treatise on the life of dreams, *The Interpretation of Dreams* offers a general theory of the mind. In this book, Freud uses his favorite research method, that is, the analysis of what we could call an altered mental state in order to arrive at a universal theory of psychic life. When Freud says, "*The interpretation of dreams is the royal road to a knowledge of the unconscious activities of the mind*" (SE 5: 608; emphasis in original), he is referring not only to the possibility of understanding his patients' psyches, but also to the fact that the study of dreams opens the possibility of understanding "normal" psychic life. In psychoanalytic theory, the difference between the normal and the pathological is economic and not structural. The psyche is the result of an economy in which quality results from the rhythmic alternations in quantities of energy, which strike at psychic organization.[12]

The study of dreams, defined as a normal psychic process, constitutes a forceful response to the claim that unconscious materials resulted from neurotic illness. The normal psyche, it was thought, was coherent and indivisibly one. But Freud's study of dreamwork demonstrated that the mechanisms deployed by neuroses and psychoses in their effort to "defend themselves" and move through the world were the same mechanisms found in dreams. For the Freudian psychoanalyst, no psychic mechanism belongs exclusively to any pathology. Quantity is what makes a qualitative difference in psychic functioning. So too, as I noted above, does the rhythm of energy's expenditure lead to qualitative differences along the path of discharge. We should not forget that the psychic apparatus is designed, in the first instance, according to the model of the reflex arc or neural pathway, whose most fundamental tendency is the search for pleasure. Likewise, for Freud, pleasure is an economic phenomenon identified with the discharge of tension: Tension is unpleasure or pain, and discharge is pleasure. But the psychic apparatus is a machine whose functioning is also much more complex than this model of excitation and relief would imply. Discharge stumbles along the path of resistance, and perception is shaped by the tissue of mnemic traces. Memory determines both the choice of a path and the rhythm of discharge, or of the relief of tension. This is what gives a sense of quality to psychic functioning. According to this theory of the mind, there are not distinct psychic structures; there are different tendencies in the discharge of energy, that is, in the search for pleasure.

In the model of the reflex arc or neural pathway, the nervous system immediately tends toward discharge, avoiding any stimulation that would alter it. This discharge has been called a "response," and in animals this response is a bodily action, a movement in space, a gesture, or the emission of sound: a reaction that seeks to avoid stimulation or alteration. But the psychic apparatus represents a mediation of this reflex. Although it is very important not to forget that according to the psychoanalytic theory of the mind, all drives will inevitably tend toward discharge, it would be a misunderstanding of psychic life to underestimate the importance of another fact: that the drive can change the object of discharge, and that this object need not be one that "naturally" corresponds to the drive. It can even, as in the case of reaction formations, be the opposite. In fact, psychic pathologies largely correspond to deviations or renunciations of the object of the drive, which result in suffering. And although, according to Freud, the discharge of a drive results in pleasure, we should not forget that the psychic apparatus is not a homogeneous and harmonic unit, but rather the site of encounters and conflicts between distinct psychic agencies, with interests and motives that are almost always at odds. This means that the satisfaction of a drive, its discharge, can cause pleasure in one sub-system but pain in another. In fact, neurosis is precisely this: a conflict of interests between distinct psychic agencies, in which the satisfaction of a desire causes pleasure in one part of the organization and suffering in another. A good analysis should therefore seek out not only the "origin" of the patient's suffering, but also the place where (or the psychic agency in which) this suffering causes pleasure. So we would not be mistaken to say that although the psyche is an apparatus designed for the discharge of the drives, it is at the same time a mechanism that allows for the postponement of this discharge, for detours, or for the attainment of substitute objects. But there is something more radical in the design of the psyche, namely that it also allows the drive to avoid discharge in the material, external world. In other words, the extraordinary thing about the psyche is that it can find satisfaction in what we might call a virtual world, one that can be external or internal. The drive can find discharge in mere thoughts, fantasies, language, creation, and dreams.

So let us return to the life of dreams. We know that the dream is a paradigmatic phenomenon for psychoanalysis, that it allows psychoanalysis to address many fundamental questions. But what I would like to underscore here is what Freud calls the "regressive path" of dreams. I have already noted (1) that it is imperative for the drive to discharge itself; and (2) that impulses normally turn to the motor system in their effort to satisfy desire. The psyche normally travels, then, from the "extreme" of perception (the registration of the stimulus) to the motor "extreme" (the path through which desire or the drive seeks to satisfy itself).

However, as I explained earlier, during dreams, desires or pulsations do not stop seeking satisfaction (or discharge), and the closure of the motor end of the psychic apparatus causes these impulses to return, causing excitation in the perception-consciousness system. Thus what unleashes the dreamwork—the imagination and oneiric fantasy—is the fact that desire cannot be satisfied through action or though the consequent modification of external reality. Is this not what culture demands of us as well? Is this not precisely the renunciation that socialization fundamentally requires? The human species has chosen to live

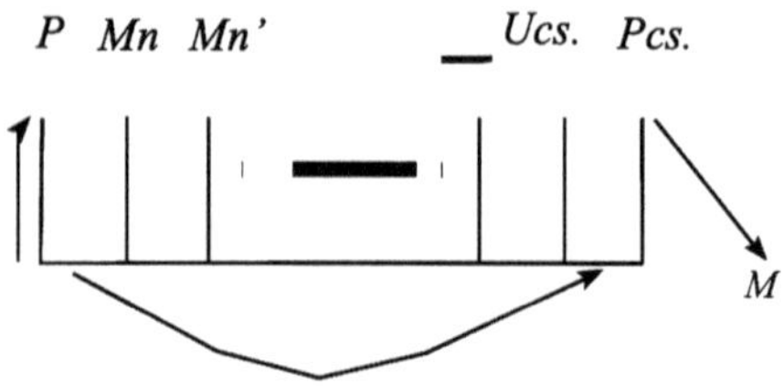

Figure 1. Freud, "comb." This is the famous "comb" graph that Freud includes in Chapter VII of *The Interpretation of Dreams* to illustrate the psyche's advancement or progress during waking life:

> We have seen that we were only to explain the formation of dreams by venturing upon the hypothesis of there being two psychical agencies, one of which submitted the activity of the other to a criticism which involved its exclusion from consciousness. The critical agency, we concluded, stands in a closer relation to consciousness than the agency criticized: it stands like a screen between the latter and consciousness. Further, we found reasons for identifying the critical agency with the agency which directs our waking life and determines our voluntary, conscious actions. If, in accordance with our assumptions, we replace these agencies by systems, then our last conclusion must lead us to locate the critical system at the motor end of the apparatus. . . .
>
> We will describe the last of the systems at the motor end as "the preconscious," to indicate that the excitatory processes occurring in it can enter consciousness without further impediment provided that certain other conditions are fulfilled: for instance, that they reach a certain degree of intensity, that the function which can only be described as "attention" is distributed in a particular way, and so on. This is at the same time the system which holds the key to voluntary movement. We will describe the system that lies behind it as "the unconscious," because it has no access to consciousness *except via the preconscious*, in passing through which its excitatory process is obliged to submit to modifications.
>
> In which of these systems, then, are we to locate the impetus to the construction of dreams? For simplicity's sake, in the system *Ucs*. It is true that in the course of our future discussion we shall learn that this is not entirely accurate, and that the process of forming dreams is obliged to attach itself to dream-thoughts belonging to the preconscious system. But when we consider the dream-wish, we shall find that the motive force for producing dreams is supplied by the *Ucs*.; and owing to this latter factor we shall take the unconscious system as the starting-point of dream-formation. Like all other thought-structures, this dream-instigator will make an effort to advance into the *Pcs*. and from there to obtain access to consciousness. (SE 5: 540–542)

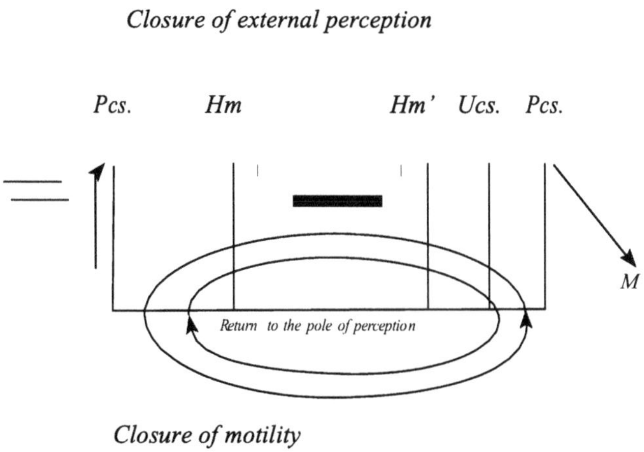

Figure 2. Arensburg and Martínez, "comb." This graph is from the Spanish psychoanalysts Bernardo Arensburg and José Guillermo Martínez. It shows an addition to Freud's comb meant to illustrate how unconscious materials—closed off from the exterior world, on one end, and from the motor system, on the other—take a regressive path and provoke hallucinatory dreams. On the regressive character of dreams, Freud explains: "The only way in which we can describe what happens in hallucinatory dreams is by saying that the excitation moves in a *backward* direction. Instead of being transmitted toward the *motor* end of the apparatus it moves toward the *sensory* end and finally reaches the perceptual system. If we describe as 'progressive' the direction taken by psychical processes arising from the unconscious during waking life, then we may speak of dreams having a 'regressive' character'" (SE 5: 542; emphasis in original).

in communities and consequently has had to sacrifice the immediate satisfaction of all desires. This renunciation gives rise to the psyche, which leads to mediation. The psyche is an apparatus for waiting, for postponement, for the transformation and substitution of objects, the distortion of messages. We should not forget that in Freud's mythology society is founded on the radical renunciation of two desires, incestuous and cannibalistic. The need not to act immediately and often not to act at all led to the construction of an internal world in which one can build castles in the air or be persecuted by monsters for the satisfaction of certain desires. When we cannot move, when we cannot act, we fantasize, imagine, and think. And the effect of our inability to accede to action is the psyche. We could even say that, like plants, we self-generate the food for our own souls.

Venturing beyond the dreamwork, Freud notes in Chapter VII of *The Interpretation of Dreams* that the regressive path taken by the pulsating energies that lead to dreams is not exclusive to them. In fact, it also explains pathological states that involve regression during waking life. Furthermore, Freud insists again that the study of these pathological states sheds light on all dreams. We are thus left with a sort of hierarchization of pathologies or extraordinary states. I am referring to the fact that in the first part of this inaugural book of psychoanalytic theory, Freud uses the study of dream mechanisms to explain psychic functioning in general; but in the second part of the book, he argues that the analysis of pathological psychic mechanisms discloses the metapsychology of dreams. So it would seem that he suggests that we can go both from pathology to dreams and from dreams to "normal" waking life. Freud writes:

> During the day there is a continuous current from the *Pcpt.* system flowing in the direction of motor activity; but this current ceases at night and could no longer form an obstacle to a current of excitation flowing in the opposite sense. Here we seem to have the "shutting-out of the external world," which some authorities regard as the theoretical explanation of the psychological characteristics of dreams.
>
> In explaining regression in dreams, however, we must bear in mind the regressions which also occur in pathological waking states; and here the explanation just given leaves us in the lurch. For in those

> cases regression occurs in spite of a sensory current flowing without interruption in a forward direction. (SE 5: 544)

Thus the difference between psychic regression in pathological states and the regression that occurs in sleep is a merely quantitative difference, a difference of degree and not of kind. Hallucinations, visions, and inner experiences that do not correspond to external reality are psychic phenomena in which energy takes a regressive path. But it seems to me that Freud did not slow down enough here to explore the theoretical consequences of the fact that in the waking life that we call normal or sane, thought, imagination, and fantasy are *also* mechanisms or means by which the psyche is redirected, following a path that leads away from movement or action. We can even say, then, that the psyche as such is the effect of a cancellation or at least of a delay in the satisfaction of the passions or vital needs, a delay that external reality imposes in the form of culture, civilization, or law. The psyche mediates between impulse and act. Here it is important to realize what kind of mediation the psyche performs. Among many others, this one stands out: thought as representation and language, since the latter is another effect of the renunciation or delay in action, a brake on the satisfaction of the drives and desires.

On the one hand, thought as representation allows us to delay or displace satisfaction. It enables us to imagine that although for the moment we cannot act on our desires (again because of the limits that reality imposes), we will be able to act later. This image of the future is what stands in the way of an immediate, unreflexive act. On the other hand, it is also true that, according to psychoanalytic theory, there is more than one way to "satisfy" or fulfill desires. There is more than dreaming and action, in other words. As Freud explains, desire can also be "sublimated," and this means that it can find fulfillment in imagination and fantasy.

Sublimation: The Creation of New, Erotic Paths for the Drive

Two claims are key for understanding psychic life from a psychoanalytic perspective. The first is the claim that, for Freud, the psyche is fundamentally an economy; the second, that the psychic apparatus operates within the domain of and is governed by the pleasure principle. Interpretations of *Beyond the Pleasure Principle* that suggest that the text describes the death drive as a force that overcomes and dethrones the pleasure principle are, to say the least, based on superficial readings of Freud. The pleasure principle is the law that governs all psychic processes. We could even risk thinking of it as a kind of "natural law" since, in *Beyond the Pleasure Principle*, Freud identifies conservatism as the universal characteristic not only of the drives—and this implies that all drives, whether they are governed by Eros or Thanatos, seek to bring about a return to a prior, inanimate state—but also of all living organisms. That is, for Freud, all living things seek out their own death, defined in Freud's treatise as the total discharge of stimulation. The psyche is thus the site of an effort to discharge tension, no matter the delay and even if this is achieved within the organization itself, that is, in the realm of the imaginary, virtual, or representational.

On the other hand, what we might call the social contract requires brutal renunciations on the part of pulsating organisms. Although these renunciations change throughout history, from a psychoanalytic point of view they always have to do with the sexual drives and the drives to destruction (where the latter are the form the death drive takes when it is directed outside the organism). Freud calls the renunciations required in social space "the reality principle." Reality is thus an obstacle that stands in the way of the desire to discharge tension.

We could say that the drive in Freud is, like the will to power in Nietzsche, reflexive. Both are forces that assert themselves inevitably, even when this means returning to their point of departure. In this sense, neurosis and the symptoms are effects of the discharge of drives that have had to find new objects, that is, that have had to renounce an object in the external world that remains inaccessible for one reason or another and have replaced it with a mental representation. So when reality, the world, or the social order prohibit the discharge of the drive, this discharge is replaced in ways that result in pathologies, with only one exception.

In "Instincts and their Vicissitudes" (1915), Freud describes the four different routes taken by the drive:

> Reversal into its opposite.
> Turning round upon the subject's own self.
> Repression.
> Sublimation.
>
> (SE 14: 126)

These are all of the routes taken by the drive, "as a measure of the demand made upon the mind for work in consequence of its connection with the body" (SE 14: 122).

But it is important that, of these four possible paths, only sublimation involves a successful transaction within the psyche's economy; that is, it is the only itinerary that circumvents repression. Although sublimation is also a defense[13] against the demands of the reality principle and the superego, it is a psychic mechanism that is not pathological. For

Freud, again, neurosis is the result of a negotiation between different psychic agencies, where the satisfaction of one of these implies pain for another. It would seem that sublimation is the only destination for the drive that manages to bring all of the layers of the psyche into agreement.

This essay or exercise in reflection on the possibility of producing a strong argument for nonviolence within psychoanalytic theory has led me to think of the psychic sublimation of the drives as a practice that, sociopolitically promoted in a way that would be in keeping with the economy of Derridean *différance*, might displace or defer the death drive or the drive to destruction. But we should analyze this hypothesis very carefully, because Freud more than once defines sublimation as a destination *only* for the sexual drives.

Freud's text on Leonardo da Vinci analyzes creativity and genius from this perspective. In this essay, Freud takes the psychic life of Leonardo as the paradigm of the sublimation of the sexual drive, rerouted into artistic production and scientific research. Freud argues that Leonardo, who to judge from biographical records did not act on his homosexuality, did not become neurotic because, instead of being repressed, his sexual impulses underwent a transformation:

> If we reflect on the concurrence in Leonardo of his over-powerful drive to research and the atrophy of his sexual life (which was restricted to what is called ideal [sublimated] homosexuality), we shall be disposed to claim him as a model instance of [sublimation]. The core of his nature, and the secret of it, would appear to be that after his curiosity had been activated in infancy in the service of sexual interest he succeeded in sublimating the greater part of his libido into an urge for research. (SE 11: 80; translation modified)

There are many tensions in Freud's text, but the most relevant for my purposes has to do with how sublimation is a path that is taken only by "the sexual impulse":

> Observation of men's daily lives shows us that most people succeed in directing very considerable portions of their sexual drive forces to their professional activity. The sexual drive is particularly well fitted to make contributions of this kind since it is endowed with a capacity for sublimation, that is, it has the power to replace its immediate aim with other aims which may be valued more highly and which are not sexual. We accept this process as proved whenever the history of a person's childhood—that is, the history of his mental development—shows that in childhood this over-powerful drive was in the service of sexual interests. We find further confirmation if a striking atrophy occurs in the sexual life of maturity, as though a portion of sexual activity had now been replaced by the activity of the over-powerful drive. (SE 11: 77–78; translation modified)

But *Leonardo da Vinci and a Memory of His Childhood* (1910) and "Instincts and Their Vicissitudes" (1915) were written before *Beyond the Pleasure Principle* (1919) and *The Ego and the Id* (1923), and it is in these latter texts that Freud devises the theory of the drives and of the structure and dynamics of the psychic apparatus. A careful reading of these two texts, *Beyond the Pleasure Principle* and *The Ego and the Id* (as well as of others, including at least *Civilization and Its Discontents*, in which we find similar formulations) lets us glimpse the possibility that the death drive might be sublimated.

Two fundamental problems must be analyzed in this context. First, both in *Beyond the Pleasure Principle* and in *The*

Ego and the Id, Freud argues that the death drive is silent and emphasizes that it always accompanies the life drive. Second, the fusion and defusion of the drives, processes that Freud describes in *The Ego and the Id*, indicate that although there are psychic phenomena in which one of the two tendencies dominates (in moments of defusion), most of the time we find the influence of both tendencies at work.

As I explained at the beginning of this chapter, in *Beyond the Pleasure Principle*, Freud posits that the primary and most primitive tendency in living organisms, the death drive, leads toward the recovery of an unaltered or inorganic state. The principle of constancy is thus nothing other than an interruption of this urge to fulfill basic physiological needs (for instance, eating, sleeping, drinking, and sex). To be alive is therefore to dwell within this tension. Eros, for Freud, is a derivative tendency:

> It can hardly be doubted that the pleasure principle serves the id as a compass in its struggle against the libido — the force that introduces disturbances into the process of life. If it is true that Fechner's principle of constancy governs life, thus consists of a continuous descent towards death, it is the claims of Eros, the sexual drives, which, in the form of needs, hold up the falling level and introduce fresh tensions. (SE 19: 46–47; translation modified)

In *The Ego and the Id*, however, Freud does not think only in terms of these two types of forces, life and death drives, but also in terms of a third that is indifferent and "displaceable," and that can lead in either deathly or erotic directions, depending on the circumstances (SE 19: 45). This undifferentiated energy is a sort of desexualized and therefore sublimated libido that "would still retain the main purpose of Eros — uniting and binding — in so far as it helps toward establishing the unity, or tendency to unity, which is particularly characteristic of the ego" (SE 19: 45).

The hypothesis regarding the existence of this third kind of energy is a typically Freudian gesture, involving the search for theoretical hypotheses to sustain his reflections despite their apparent contradictions. In Freud's words: "We have reckoned as though there existed in the mind—whether in the ego or in the id—a displaceable energy, which, neutral in itself, can be added to a qualitatively differentiated erotic or destructive impulse, and augment its total cathexis. Without assuming the existence of a displaceable energy of this kind we can make no headway" (SE 19: 44).

Freud adds: "For the opposition between the two classes of drives we may put the polarity of love and hate" (SE 19: 42; translation modified). Elsewhere he writes that "hate changes into love and love into hate" (SE 19: 43). This means that a deathly or destructive impulse can be transformed into an erotic one and in this way sublimated. But we should also note that in almost every form of human expression in which libidinal energy takes the path of sublimation, we can find shades of Thanatos. It is clear that a work of art, for example, can also be an object that evokes violence, aggression, death, and destruction. Or we can think of street demonstrations, where demands and protests can take aggressive forms. What I mean is that it is impossible to think of a product of, or an act mediated by, the psyche that would be either purely erotic or purely deathly. Freud already knew this in *Beyond the Pleasure Principle*, and he repeats it in *The Ego and the Id*: "On this view, a special physiological process (of anabolism or catabolism) would be associated with each of the two classes of drives; both kinds of drives would be active in every particle of living substance, though in unequal proportions, so that some one substance might be the principal representative of Eros" (SE 19: 41).

I deduce from this passage that the death drive, when it accompanies an erotic drive that is sublimated, loses both its potency and its immediacy. This means that psychic mediation in the form of thought, creation, or linguistic expression manages to lend the destructive drive a force such that, although it is affirmed in the world (or directed back on itself, as in superegoic reproach), it does not become annihilating and can be metabolized. Recall that, already in Chapter 1, I explained at length that the destructive drive can also have erotic effects, where what is destroyed is precisely not what gives complexity to life or existence, but what leads it toward simplicity, indifference, or destruction.

Time and again, Freud repeats the claim that the sexual drives are more plastic and more easily redirected than destructive drives. But he never offers an explanation. He mentions the fact that when it is interrupted by Eros and the conservative instincts, the death drive is neutralized and redirected outward through the motor or muscular system (SE 19: 41). From this perspective, the only thing that is indispensable for the drive is the goal, that is, the aim of satisfaction. It is for this reason that Freud points to the possibility of its displacement and transmutation. We could say that there is a certain indifference about the path taken and the object of discharge, because the drive's priority is simply to ensure that discharge takes place.

The sublimation of the destructive drives is therefore more complex and less frequent than the sublimation of the sexual drives, but still possible. Such sublimation is possible because, on one hand, as I have already indicated, the drive cannot change its aim, but it can change both the path it takes and its object; and, on the other hand, the psyche is capable of transferring—or rather, it is perhaps even the essence of the psyche to transfer—affect and the discharge of the drives from one object to another. In fact, these two characteristics of psychic life are what make psychoanalysis possible as a clinical practice and cure. We should not forget that psychoanalytic treatment seeks first to transform any neurosis into a matter of transference; in other words, therapeutic work encourages the pathology to "play" within analytic space, and encourages the patient to take the figure of the analyst as an object. Once this goal has been achieved, the work consists of the analysis of the transference, and Freud argues that the cure depends on this precisely. It is very significant that, for example, when he considers sublimation, Freud recalls a scene that has nothing to do with the erotic or with artistic creation, but has to do instead with a violent death:

> Not long ago Rank published some good examples of the way in which neurotic acts of revenge can be directed against the wrong people. Such behavior on the part of the unconscious reminds one of the comic story of the three village tailors, one of whom had to be hanged because the only village blacksmith had committed a capital offense. Punishment must be exacted even if it does not fall upon the guilty. (SE 19: 45)

In Mexico, there is a saying that goes: "It doesn't matter who wronged me, but it matters who pays [*no importa quién me la hizo sino quién me la pague*]." Both this saying and Freud's anecdote refer, I think, to the possibility that the destructive drive might change both its path and its object. In what follows, I would like to argue that, inasmuch as the psyche itself is the effect of the delay of the drive's discharge and the effect of its mediation, imagined objects, representations of reality, language, and thought are all means by which the drive might be reduced or objects onto which it can be displaced or at least deferred in its satisfaction. This implies that the drive's movements might be distributed and the force of its discharge lessened. In Freud's words: "If thought-processes in the wider sense are to be included among these displacements, then the activity of thinking is also supplied from the sublimation of erotic motive forces" (SE 19: 45). Finally, sublimation, like neurosis and the symptom, implies a psychic capacity to replace an external object of desire with a work of fiction. But in sublimation, the objects are also highly socially valued.

I have insisted that sublimation implies a displacement, and I would like to recall here that displacement is also one of the fundamental mechanisms of dreamwork. In *The Interpretation of Dreams*, Freud indicates that there are two such mechanisms: condensation and displacement. In the former, the psyche imbues a sign with very different meanings; in the latter, the meaning of one sign is grafted onto another. But isn't this what thinking does in general? Doesn't thinking imply mediation in the form of postponement and delay? Doesn't all representation involve the displacement of the affects, a movement from external reality to mental objects? Thinking, understood as representation, involves precisely these two psychic mechanisms, since the work of thought is a work of imbuing signs with meaning and with affect, and of grafting meanings and affects onto signs.

But displacement and condensation are not the only mechanisms that thinking and the dreamwork share. What facilitates dreaming is the drive's inability to find an outlet in motor action. Since the aim of the drive, its effort to find an outlet, cannot be renounced, it discharges itself within the psychic apparatus itself. Freud calls this the "regressive" character of dreams. But this regression can take place despite the fact that there is at the same time a quantity of energy coursing through the muscular system: "[R]egression occurs in spite of a sensory current flowing without interruption in a forward direction" (SE 5: 544). This means that it is not only in pathologies and in dreams that psychic energy flows toward the perception-consciousness system, but also in psychic processes in which the secondary process is operative, as in imagination and thought.

When we are asleep, we cannot move or act with the aim of bringing about modifications in the external world in order to placate the drive. But culture also prevents us from acting on many of our desires, so we fantasize, imagine, and dream. Sublimation advances toward spaces outside the psychic organization, without its objects being displaced immediately. By this I do not mean that the results of sublimation do not affirm the real world. I mean instead that, in spatiotemporal terms, when desire is displaced from a material object in external reality toward a fictional object, or grafted onto such a fictional object, psychic mediation takes up time and space whether or not this process results in a materialization of the idea or re-presentation of desire,[14] as in artistic works or discursive acts, for example. All sublimating action is virtual; this appears to be an oxymoron, but in fact it is not. It points rather to the necessity of understanding the materiality or materialization of the virtual. In other words, it is a matter of understanding space as necessarily virtual *and* material. The psyche shows us that space is undecidable, at once virtual and material.

But this is not an easy task, first because not all representations are erotic (as in dreams, there are anxieties and other affects that give rise to suffering); and second, because in order for sublimation to take place, psychic mechanisms must be very sophisticated. Like houseplants — domestic or rather domesticated plants — psychic mechanisms must be cultivated and fed very carefully. Sublimation requires loving care and the sowing of powerful seeds that can generate creative and productive ideas, nurturing their growth. This is an enormous social effort. And I would like to underscore the social character of this labor, because just as houseplants must be fed by someone who also ensures that they are given adequate light and water, we are domestic and domesticated creatures, and our souls must be fed by others.

We must not forget that, as I indicated above, the greatest difficulty in psychic life derives from the fact that the drive can change its object, even to the point of bringing an object into being, but it cannot *not* seek its own satisfaction or, in energetic terms, the discharge of its tension. Reading Freud with Nietzsche—or perhaps reading Freud as he rewrites Nietzsche—we can see that the drive is a will to power and the psyche a matter of bad conscience that turns the drive back on itself. Of course this does not mean that the drive is not ultimately discharged in the world at any time, or even in the majority of cases. But it does mean that the psyche is produced by a discharge that is not immediate, a discharge of the drive in the body itself and in representation. The psyche, in other words, is the mechanism by which the world becomes an image.

It is the psyche's task to facilitate the delay of the drive's satisfaction, but never to bring about its renunciation. The radical impossibility of silencing desire can lead efforts to renounce it onto the terrain of pathology. The psyche must be capable of imagining that desire will be fulfilled some time, because imagination and thought are precisely matters of spatiotemporal mediation. Recall that not all drives can be satisfied or placated, because some threaten the social order itself (as in the cases of incest and cannibalism, to mention those that, for Freud, gave rise to the first Western political organizations). The public sphere should therefore offer substitute objects, substitute satisfactions. The effort to eliminate all satisfactions of desire can only lead to pathological pain.

Thinking in social terms can help us shed light on the region that I would like to illuminate. Poverty and social marginalization are obvious examples of the ways in which the world presents itself to certain people as a place that makes the fulfillment of certain needs and desires radically impossible. Poor and marginalized people cannot imagine that their desires will be fulfilled sometime in the future, because the social order has closed off this future, their future. Under these conditions, some criminal acts point to a particular logic (one that is also perverse, to be sure). I am thinking, for instance, of the hundreds of young people in Mexico who have joined the ranks of gangs and drug-trafficking cartels. As long as the state cannot offer these citizens possibilities for the fulfillment of their needs or the realization of their aspirations, it will be easy for these young people to enter organized crime. Although gangs will not offer them long lives, they at least offer their members something approaching what they have imagined as happiness. The Mexican state has been unable to offer young people either an enjoyable, fulfilling future or the space for hope, which would require schools and recreational activities and would create the conditions for what Freud calls the sublimation of desires. In this way, sublimation might be understood as a conservative or even reactionary mechanism, in which the need for a loaf of bread would be supplanted or fulfilled by the reading of poem. But I am not referring to any such displacements, which would be as absurd as they are impossible. As in every economy, in the psyche some equivalences are possible, and others are not. I would argue, then, that erotic sublimation, the kind that creates new paths and opens new horizons, cannot be thought of as conservative, for these same reasons.[15]

The psyche is an economy in which we could say two different currencies circulate. According to Freud, when transactions that lead to pleasurable experiences outnumber others, this leads to a "balance" that makes it possible for us to bear the discontent deriving from our inability to satisfy our most radical desires. If this is the case, then the psyche is a medium (in the sense of a medium of exchange) that manages to produce happiness, or "lives worthy of being lived." At the same time, however, the psychic organism must maintain a certain quantity of tension in order to stay alive In other words, life entails delayed satisfaction. The psyche, understood as the result of a confrontation between a biological organization and the world, is an economy that never arrives at the point of full resolution between the different agencies and tendencies that constitute it. The human being dwells in, develops in, and is this confrontation. On the one hand, this human being has decided to live in society and civilization in order to stay alive or "in" life. But this life is neither pure nor full; that is, it has had to sacrifice part of itself. Civilization has demanded very painful renunciations. From a psychoanalytic point of view, the insatiable structure of desire is the effect of the prohibition on the fulfillment of the desires that are primary and primitive. It is because of this voraciousness that we must think of the paths that slow down and circumvent the demand of deathly desires as these seek to affirm themselves. But let us return to the excessive nature of these embattled tendencies, because it is also vitally important to understand that the opposing forces that, for Freud, account for the functioning of the psychic apparatus—the pleasure principle and the reality principle, the sexual drives and drives toward self-preservation, Eros and Thanatos—are all related in that their confrontation with one another causes a tension that does not result in the neutralization of either impulse, but rather ignites both.

So let us consider life's renunciation of an essential part of itself, of certain desires that cannot be satisfied within the framework of civilization without resulting in a return to barbarism. But if, on the one hand, the desire for destruction is never eliminated, so that efforts to domesticate it can never let their guard down, on the other, these efforts are condemned to failure. Still, although the task of culture is impossible, unrealizable, it must be performed. And doing this work makes sense, because as long as we do it, we delay the satisfaction of humanity's selfish desires (endogamous desires, cannibalistic desires, and desires for the destruction of the other, whether in the name of self-defense or merely out of cruelty, which is to say for the pleasure of causing pain). Culture is in this sense a detour, a meandering path, a circuitous route that will ultimately lead us to death. But the pause, the parenthesis along the way, can be radically erotic and can also be postponed for later if possible. What we need is thus a map of the path or detour. This has not been working out, and rather than providing us with a map of paths through the wild, civilization has paved one-way streets to destruction.

Beyond the economy of forces that are at the "origin" of life, and given that, as I explained in Chapter 1, there is no life without the processes of alteration that are brought to bear on another, previous organization, life is beset by a drive that we could call a drive to sovereignty that forgets its own heteronomous genesis. (Freud and Derrida call this the drive to dominate or cruelty.) Culture is thus a double-edged sword: on the one hand, if we want to live in society, we have no choice but to sacrifice a certain form of sovereignty, and this abdication, according to Freud, leads to discontent. On the other hand, however, from a psychoanalytic point of view, culture would also seem to be the only means by which we might overcome the discontent of civilization that is culture itself. In Ricoeur's words: "This paradox continues into the higher stages of civilized life: a strange struggle indeed, for civilization kills us in order to make us live, by using, for itself and against us, the sense of guilt, while at the same time we must loosen its embrace in order to live and find enjoyment" (323). We must not forget that culture includes not only language, art, gastronomy, and the whole erotic realm — all of which we might think of as the products of human efforts to understand the enigma of life — but also rules and laws and certain habits, customs, and practices that misrecognize or even annihilate other forms of life.

As Marcuse writes in his inspiring text *Eros and Civilization*, the reality principle is historical, and therefore we could say that there are reality principles and reality principles. Marcuse takes as his point of departure the claim that Freud does not make the correct and necessary distinction between the biological vicissitudes of the instincts and their sociohistorical fate; Marcuse introduces two new concepts into psychoanalytic theory, in an effort to draw attention to this distinction. He distinguishes, on the one hand, between basic repression and surplus repression; and, on the other hand, between the reality principle and the performance principle:

> [E]very form of the reality principle must be embodied in a system of societal institutions and relations, laws and values which transmit and enforce the required "modification" of the instincts. This "body" of the reality principle is different at different stages of civilization. Moreover, while any form of the reality principle demands a considerable degree and scope of repressive control over the instincts, the specific historical institutions of the reality principle and the specific interests of domination introduce *additional* controls over and above those indispensable for civilized human association. These additional controls

> arising from the specific institutions of domination are what we denote as *surplus repression*. (37)

Pointing to the sociohistorical character of the performance principle implies that this principle can be modified through political work and of course through erotic work as well. The contradictory project of civilization can be defined as a negotiation between what we might, in biological terms, call the selfish gene and the altruistic gene, or between an absolutely narcissistic impulse that tends toward its own death and an impulse toward association and the construction of ever more complex forms of organization. This project is reanimated anew at every moment and in every cultural act or effect. Culture and civilization are thus at once an affront and a kind of salvation.

As I noted earlier, if the human being were to satisfy its most radical desires, then the psyche—at least the psyche as we know it—would collapse, because the psyche is itself the effect of an encounter and negotiation (obviously, most often an unsuccessful negotiation) between the drives and the law that prohibits their direct fulfillment. A further problem remains unaddressed, however, and it is at once inspiring and fundamental. I am referring to the fact that culture itself is the effect of a prohibition. Here, however, we cannot write a linear history of culture and the psyche. As a semiotic function, culture is the product of unsatisfied desires. In other words, frustration is the condition of possibility for symbolization:

> Moreover, if man could be satisfied, he would be deprived of something more important than pleasure—symbolization, which is the counterpart of dissatisfaction. Desire, qua insatiable demand, gives rise to speech. The semantics of desire, which we are focussing upon here, is bound up with this postpone-

ment of satisfaction, with this endless mediating of pleasure. (Ricoeur 322)

Freud calls the sufferings that are traceable to the social contract civilization's discontents. But it turns out that, elliptically, the only route, or rather the only detour, for the discharge of the drive that does not lead to pathology is work within the symbolic order. In other words, the form of displeasure caused by human beings' introduction to civilization opens onto an aporia: How is it that the path to happiness and harmony is also the path that leads to discontent? That is, for *homo sapiens*, happiness and discontent are both found in culture. On one hand, it is clear that in order to argue for such a paradox, Freud must mean more than one thing by "culture." On the other hand, we will see that the origin of the semantic is found in frustration. Culture is thus a place in the world that makes extremely urgent demands on the individual, but it is also a place that allows the individual to be divided in two, to occupy a place above these demands and to bypass them. (I will return below to humor, defined as a semantic and superegoic capacity that allows for the surreptitious liberation of affect that was originally painful and associated with representation, but is turned into hilarity.)[16] All of this is possible because culture—all of culture—is a semiotic function, that is, a system of signification. Signification is the fundamental mechanism of culture (Eco, *A Theory of Semiotics* 22).

Language and Negation

In her text "The Impudence of Uttering: Mother Tongue," Julia Kristeva argues that language, defined not as the object of modern linguistics, but as a semiotic practice, a cultural phenomenon, is the royal road to sublimation:

> [I]t is through language that *sublimation* is intrinsically and inevitably cultural, in the sense that it is a bearer of creativity, which is precisely what distinguishes it from *repression* and *idealization*. I say, *through language*, and by this I mean language not as an object of such and such a branch of modern or traditional linguistics, but as a semiotic practice open to the heterogeneity of drives: an enunciation, if you like, thanks to which the alchemy of pleasure transforms into *jouissance*, and the symbolic bond into creativity. (n.p.)

In chemistry, the phenomenon known as sublimation involves the direct passage of matter from a solid to a gaseous state, without passing through the liquid state. In the psychic realm, when the sexual drive is sublimated, this means that it is satisfied or fulfilled without passing through sexuality. As we know from Freud's text on Leonardo, it was not only the natural sciences that inspired Freud to name this defense mechanism "sublimation"; he wanted the name to resonate with the aesthetic sublime as well. This psychic transaction is a sort of exchange of currencies, an exchange made with the aim of acquiring one thing: pleasure. The "currency" of sexuality is converted into the "currency" of sublime production. Fundamental here is the fact that the drive's new aim and new object are both socially valued. In other words, if the drive has been sublimated, this means its aim is no longer sexual, and its object is culturally valorized. In Freud's words: "A certain kind of modification of the aim and change of the object, in which our social valuation is taken into account, is described by us as 'sublimation'" (SE 22: 97). In her discussion of sublimation, Kristeva concurs in thinking of the economy of pleasure as involving a kind of alchemy. And to be sure, when, in this transaction, motor discharge, which can affect the world in a direct or immediate manner, is sublimated, as in chemistry, the drive—or libidinal "substance"—evaporates, becoming representation. This means that sublimation always takes place on the terrain of the "as if," that is, in the realm of metaphor, no matter the degree of naturalization or sedimentation that it is up against. As a semiotic function, language turns objects and actions into mere "breath."

The detour that sublimation takes passes through narcissism, but it continues past this point. We have seen that, in the experience of satisfaction, there is a return to primary narcissism, which must be overcome if the organism is to stay alive. Although it is true that neither hallucinations nor representations can meet basic needs, and there is a limit to this economy of pleasure (and the equivalence of the currencies exchanged), what I would like to underscore here is the radical importance of the moment of mediation. I also want to emphasize the possibility that, under certain conditions, and under the pressure of certain desires, one object can be substituted for another and the latter can even be virtual.

It is clear, then, that if the organism chooses life, it must renounce certain regressive circuits during waking life. Nevertheless, this renunciation is limited, circumscribed by specific demands and calculations within the social world. There are two fundamental problems that need to be underscored here. First, although they are regressive, dreams and language involve the discharge of the drive. And second, it would seem that all of the mechanisms related to the sublime run counter to progress, that is, that they are not directed toward immediate action, but rather toward forms of discharge involving representations or psychic mediation. The return to primary narcissism implies an inversion of the libido, now directed toward a mnemic trace. A psychic trace has been taken as an object, and in this moment a possibility is born: the possibility that action can evaporate in language.

In all psychic phenomena involving the objectification of a mnemic trace — that is, all psychic phenomena in which such a trace becomes the object of the drive's discharge — action dissipates. It enters a virtual world, though this world is still a world in Hannah Arendt's sense: It is unique to the human condition. Clearly there are regressive paths that lead in pathological directions — toward the neurotic symptom or psychotic hallucinations, to name only two obvious examples. But then what is the difference between these paths and those created in sublimation? Why do some lead to pain and others to pleasure? Essentially, sublimation and dreams involve psychic transactions that are completely successful. By contrast, in neurosis and psychosis, Freud says, one psychic agency experiences a satisfaction that at the same time implies pain for another psychic agency.

Given all of this, we can now see that language is the supplement by which the subject is "subjected" to civilizing law. But language is also this subject's only tool for going beyond this law's urgent demands for renunciation, into the world of the sublime. Language, as Derrida would say following Plato, is a *pharmakon* that is at once medicine and poison, undecidably. According to Freud, basic bodily necessities — here hunger is the paradigmatic example — are what modify the psyche's primary tendency to avoid all stimulation (in keeping with the model of the reflex arc or neural path). In the example of satisfying hunger, the infant creates a trace of the image of the person who repeatedly feeds it, and who will then be the one called every time hunger presents itself. But in order for this mechanism to be established, hunger must first be repeatedly satisfied. That is, in order for the mnemic trace to be registered or inscribed as such, the line or path must be laid down more than once.

After the infant has experienced satisfaction and established an association between a bodily need—hunger, in this example—and the elimination of that need, the next time the need arises, Freud says:

> [A] psychical impulse will at once emerge which will seek to re-cathect the mnemic image of the perception and to re-evoke the perception itself, that is to say, to re-establish the situation of the original satisfaction. An impulse of this kind is what we call a wish [*deseo* in the Spanish]; the reappearance of the perception is the fulfillment of the wish [*deseo*]. (SE 5: 565–566)

In order for the infant to recall the image not only of being fed but of the one who feeds it, this process must be repeated numerous times. That is, the infant can cling to such an image and seek out such a perception in the external world if and only if the experience has been repeated. This repetition is thus what creates the experience of satisfaction, and this experience is what sets the psychic apparatus in motion in such a way that it can abandon merely reflexive functioning and perform more complex and sophisticated functions. This detour taken by the psychic apparatus as it seeks to fulfill its wish or desire is nothing other than a work of thought. Until this moment in its psychic development, the infant has not cathected the world; its nascent mind has only created an image of the person who brings relief. For a period whose duration is unknown—but presumably short in human beings who are "healthy"—what the infant seeks in order to satisfy itself is this image rather than any object. This period continues in primary narcissism, that is, in the state (which for Freud is primordial and original) in which every organism seeks relief in itself.

For Marcuse, however, primary narcissism is not just a

stage in libidinal development, but a specific way of relating to external reality, in which the nascent ego becomes one with the world. This interpretation is extremely interesting for many reasons, but the most important in this context is that this Narcissus, rather than selfishly relating to external reality, merges with it. According to Marcuse, this relation implies an erotic renunciation of the love of objects, but it also implies an association with a more complex Eros, which binds one to the universe:

> Indeed, the discovery of primary narcissism meant more than the addition of just another phase to the development of the libido; with it there came in sight the archetype of another existential relation to *reality*. Primary narcissism is more than autoeroticism; it engulfs the "environment," integrating the narcissistic ego with the objective world. The normal antagonistic relation between ego and external reality is only a later form and stage of the relation between ego and reality. (*Eros* 168)

Now, narcissism is also a form of resistance to subordination by the law. This can take the form either of becoming one with the law or of refusing to recognize it. Here the result can be pathological, and this is not merely a matter of quantity (as opposed to structure). Like all regressive circuits in the psyche, narcissism involves gains in pleasure that result from holding oneself above the law. But according to Marcuse, narcissism is also decisive for sublimation:

> In *The Ego and the Id*, [Freud] asks "whether all sublimation does not take place through the agency of the ego, which begins by changing sexual object-libido and then, perhaps, goes on to give it another aim." If this is the case, then all sublimation would begin with

> the reactivation of narcissistic libido, which somehow overflows and extends to objects. (169)

In short, the original and primary narcissistic impulse creates the route that all psychic regressions, and all forms of sublimation, will follow. Thus the recourse to an image, idea, or fantasy to fulfill a wish or satisfy a desire always leaves a trace.

We could say that, in Freud, although the philosophical category of the subject is not a category that he works with, the subject comes into being when it recognizes the difference between the world and its mnemic representation. Freud writes: "Thought is after all nothing but a substitute for a hallucinatory wish [*deseo* in the Spanish]" (SE 5: 567). In effect, thinking is the detour that the psychic apparatus must take in order to keep the organism alive; to this end, it must turn toward the "exterior." This turning, for Freud, is the psychic work of thought.

Nevertheless, Kristeva explains:

> [I]t is not enough to say that language defends itself against sexual desire and the movement of drives by giving them a psychic representation and inverting them: drive energy becomes the investment and it is the mnesiac trace which is "objectalized" (A. Green), on top of or sometimes in place of the erotic object. Indeed, the psychic inscription never stops acting, being active and thus energetic, by doubly reversing itself: toward its energetic source and towards its own opposite direction, to preserve desire like a secret around which the psychic identity clusters . . . (n.p.)

In other words, certain semiotic operations make it possible for the drive to discharge itself in representation and attain complete satisfaction.

Language as remedy (re-mediation), like all semiotic ties, is ambivalent in that it can be an apparatus of power that subjects us and at the same time, paradoxically, lead us beyond this subjection. Language is thus a cultural supplement that allows for creativity and the conservation of social ties. It is the royal road of eroticism. Kristeva writes: "Language is an utterance which signals to sexualization . . . while disburdening it by the simple fact that it names instead of acting" (n. p.; translation modified).

Language is therefore a product of sublimation, and in this sense there is no language without creativity. But language is not only a matter of the kind of sublimation in which the act evaporates and enters the virtual realm; language itself has a fictional structure. Language is an "as if." It is as if the thing were present in its phonetic or written representation. This is why Kristeva argues that language is a fetish, because the word as representation of the thing cannot be thought of as anything other than a cultural perversion that is constitutive of the human species. Recall that, for Freud, fetishism is the paradigm of all perversion, and that its privileged defense is disavowal. In this mechanism, the psyche knows—in the sense that it has conscious access to a displaced representation registered in the psychic organization—what it at the same time refuses to know. The paradigmatic fetishist in Freud's text on the topic is a pervert who denies the fact of female castration, playing with objects that he fetishizes: lingerie, high heels, and other objects that we might think of as "manufactured sex." His analysis of the meaning of these objects leads Freud to the conclusion that they are substitutes for the phallus, something that allows the pervert to behave psychically as if the woman did have a penis. What I would like to highlight here is the fictional and playful element of fetishism, that is, the figure of the "as if" that is the same here as in any other fantasy, hallucination, dream, or word:

> Always already transposed by language in culture, one is indefinitely working through polymorphous perversity in creativity. Speaking beings have no other creativity than that which finds languages to carry out this "auto-re-creation" of the self we call psychic life. (Kristeva n.p.; translation modified)

From this perspective, language is a double disavowal, an acting "as if" twice over: not a denial of reality, but a granting of the status of reality to an illusion. I am referring to the illusion produced by the word. This is an exercise in hyperreality, then, in which words become things. And we should not forget that words also produce effects that are material, as in the case of insults or the naming of gender, which shapes both bodies and psyches. In these acts of interpellation, the subject affirms its guilt or acts as if it is the one being addressed. Performative language occupies a hybrid space in this description. When we "do things with words," as J. L. Austin says, as in forgiving, promising, ordering, offending, or flattering, we are discharging energy in directions that are at once progressive and regressive.

Given all of the above, we would not be wrong to argue that everything in the psychological realm is in a certain sense regressive. If the external world and the public sphere are not modified by immediate action, psychic energy is at least partly discharged in a regressive way. But of course, as I noted earlier, there are regressive paths that are pathological and others that are erotic, some that tend toward destruction and others that facilitate and help us seek out socialization.

The animality of the human being, which the psychoanalytic notion of the drive sought to rescue from forgetting, is diluted somewhat, or complicated, if we remember that human's status as a speaking being. Regressive or mediated paths toward the discharge of the drive resemble the image of a tree that grows into numerous branches, rather than the image of a hunting tiger running through the jungle, stepping on and destroying everything that stands in its way. By this I do not mean that we should simply "shelve" or seek to move beyond the question of the animal and its relation to the "rationality" or the "sickness" of the human animal. This would be to repeat a move made countless times in anthropological (and anthropocentric) thought. But we should not forget that desires for coexistence have led human beings toward other ways of living in the world. What we might call a reconciliation with the irrationality and willfulness of the animals that we are still cannot displace the problem of the animal that we are *not*. Nor can such a reconciliation function as an alibi for human violence. So just as the metaphor of the animal has been very productive for political thought, turning to plants—like the tree to which I have just referred—might allow us to reflect on the renunciation of the animal and the drive that civilization and culture demand of *homo sapiens*. In other words, the possibilities for thought and for symbolization, broadly defined, that are opened by culture might lead us into a realm that resembles the plant kingdom rather than that of the animal.

On the one hand, the metaphysical and anthropological traditions have privileged the capacity for movement as one of the fundamental features differentiating animals from plants. On the other hand, culture has functioned to delay human fulfillment, to slow down our movement toward the fulfillment of the drives by rerouting them through thought, imagination, and artistic production. It is thus interesting to ask whether human beings might be animals that have been made into plants by culture. In short, the space opened up by culture, which mediates between the drive and its fulfillment, depends on the elimination of immediate action, an elimination that makes thought, imagination, and fantasy possible.

From this point of view, it would seem that we have forgotten—that is, that we have stopped thinking about—our botanical inheritance as *homo sapiens*. The philosophical tradition has been seduced by the Aristotelian definition of the species as the rational animal. It is as if philosophy had to follow the lead of biology, thinking of evolutionary time as chronological or thinking of the development of life in terms of *zoe* and not *bios*. I am referring to the fact that we have thought of ourselves as animals because these are the biological relatives that are closest to us in linear time. We have followed the classificatory scheme that suggests that what defines us is the chronological moment of our appearance on Earth. We are more animal than plant, by this account, because we share more genetic information with animals, and because we appeared on the planet just after the animals to whom we are genetically closest. All of these are facts that it would be stupid to deny. But it is important to ask why these "hard facts" are those that govern not only our place in taxonomies of life, but also philosophical, anthropological, and sociopolitical definitions of the human being. It seems to me that it is at least interesting to ask if chronological time and geo-centrism might not be the best parameters for thinking the human conditions.

How does culture or civilization constrain human beings? It seems to me that the answer to this question can be stated this way: Culture prevents action without delay. And, for psychoanalysis, the effect of this displacement or postponement of action is precisely the psyche. In his essay "Negation," Freud addresses a significant dimension of the sublimating function of language (perhaps without fully realizing the extent of the horizon opened up by this simple psychic operation). Fundamentally, negation is a defense mechanism that allows for the irruption of repressed material into consciousness, on the condition that the affirmation of the object is inverted, becoming a negation. In his essay, Freud indicates that, confronted with a negation in the patient's discourse, the analyst must follow the path traced by this negative enunciation until reaching a psychic inscription. For Freud, this path inevitably shows that negation is an obstacle standing in the way of a repressed mnemic trace. Negation is the sign of a refused drive.

According to Freud, the linguistic function of negation is traceable to the oral and anal stages of psychic development. Oral and anal forms of sexual pleasure are associated with the psychic capacity to devour or expel loved objects, respectively. That is, these stages give rise to the symbol of negation, and this transmutation of sexuality into its representation—the representation of the incorporation of the desired object or the expulsion of the bothersome object—is the royal road to sublimation. In Freud's words:

> The function of judgment is concerned in the main with two sorts of decisions. It affirms or disaffirms the possession by a thing of a particular attribute; and it asserts or disputes that a presentation has an existence in reality. The attribute to be decided about may originally have been good or bad, useful or harmful. Expressed in the language of the oldest—the oral—instinctual impulses, the judgment is: "I should like to eat this," or "I should like to spit it out"; and, put more generally: "I should like to take this inside of myself and to keep that out." That is to say: "It shall be inside me" or "it shall be outside me." As I have shown elsewhere, the original pleasure-ego wants to introject into itself everything that is good and to

> eject from itself everything that is bad. What is bad, what is alien to the ego, and what is external are, to begin with identical.
>
> The other sort of decision made by the function of judgment—as to the real existence of something of which there is a presentation (reality-testing)—is a concern of the definitive reality-ego, which develops out of the initial pleasure-ego. It is now no longer a question of whether what has been perceived (a thing) shall be taken into the ego or not, but of whether something which is in the ego as a presentation can be rediscovered in perception (reality) as well. It is, we see, once more a question of *external* and *internal*. (SE 19: 236–237)

Negation is a mechanism worthy of Melville's Bartleby, then, in that

> [t]o negate something in a judgment is, at bottom, to say: "This is something which I should prefer to repress." A negative judgment is the intellectual substitute for repression; its "no" is the hall-mark of repression, a certificate of origin—like, let us say, "Made in Germany." With the help of the symbol of negation, thinking frees itself from the restrictions of repression and enriches itself with material that is indispensable for its proper functioning. (SE 19: 236)

Freud traces the origins of the intellectual function of reality testing back to the very first moments of human life. He shows that the negation of an object begins when psychic functioning is governed by the pleasure principle. The primitive psyche is a narcissistic organization in two senses: first, in that it identifies everything good as part of its own structure; and, second, because it does not recognize external reality.

The intellectual capacity for judgment is a reality test whose function is to differentiate between the representation of the object, on the one hand, and, on the other, the object in the external world. Memory does not keep an analogue record of the object, and the discordances between the object and its representation allow the subject to differentiate between the external and the internal, and to distinguish between the experiences of satisfaction that they offer. Reality testing takes place when the object is absent, and the psyche must therefore have recourse to its representation. When the latter does not relieve its pain, the infant recognizes that the object of satisfaction is elsewhere, in the external world. In this experience, narcissism suffers its first disappointment. (Moreover, this experience is a door through which one enters the realm of neurosis, leaving the realm of psychosis.)

These two sets of experiences—of satisfaction, on the one hand, and, on the other, of the aftermath of primary narcissism, when the psyche seeks to banish from consciousness everything that causes pain and to incorporate everything that causes pleasure—pave the way for reality testing, pointing to the terrain on which it will take place. We could say that what Freud is indicating in "Negation" is that judgment is negative at first, that is, that its first formulations take the form of rejections: The paradigmatic infant recognizes the external world not by affirming it, but by negating the image in its head, which cannot be the source of pleasure. In other words, the first judgment is something like, "this image does not feed me," and not, "this object feeds me." Judgment thus originates in negation, defined as the expulsion of everything that the psychic organization does not want to take in, of everything that does not help it to survive.

Yet the intellect is not the same as consciousness. Consciousness is the intellect understood as a capacity for judgment plus a perceptual system. Like perception, consciousness cannot avoid all of the unpleasure resulting from experiences that come from without, because its protection against stimulation does not always offer sufficient resistance. But in addition, the forces that safeguard repression are not, for the most part, powerful enough to prevent offshoots of the repressed from irrupting in consciousness. So negation shows that it is possible to bypass repression without causing pain in consciousness.

According to Freud, this psychic mechanism divides idea from affect:

> Thus the content of a repressed image or idea can make its way into consciousness, on the condition that it is *negated*. Negation is a way of taking cognizance of what is repressed; indeed, it is already a lifting of the repression, though not, of course, an acceptance of what is repressed. We can see how in this the intellectual function is separated from the affective process. (SE 19: 235–236)

Negation therefore allows repressed material to accede to consciousness while blocking the entry of the corresponding affect. What is rejected in and through negation is the feeling associated with a specific representation. In clinical terms, this psychic procedure indicates what is repressed, but at the same time it also points to the body subjected by the superego and the affect that follows from this subordination.

Negation thus fulfills two contradictory functions simultaneously. On the one hand, it is already an overcoming of repression in that the repressed material of the unconscious manages to enter consciousness. But on the other hand, negation suppresses the affect corresponding to this material, which remains unconscious. Jean Hyppolite notes of this process: "This seems very profound to me. If the psychoanalyzed person accepts this, he goes back on his negation and yet the repression is still there! I conclude from this that one must give what happens here a philosophical name, a name Freud did not pronounce: negation of the negation" ("Spoken Commentary" 883). Negation and the function of judgment are also signs that the subject is capable of taking a certain distance from the displeasing consequences caused by the incursion of repressed material into consciousness—and, Freud adds, those caused by the compulsion of the pleasure principle as well. This is, I think, the essence of negation: If repressed judgment enters consciousness, then, as Freud says, it does so as the cancellation of a repression, but also at the same time as a sort of sublimation, because the repressed material enters consciousness in a desexualized form and without causing pain. Once the role of negation is explained in these terms, we must then also explain how it makes a detour around the compulsion to repeat.

We have seen that, on the one hand, language is the royal road to sublimation, and, on the other, that negation is a semiotic function. Freud explains near the end of "Negation" that, in chronological terms:

> The study of judgment affords us, perhaps for the first time, an insight into the origin of an intellectual function from the interplay of the primary instinctual impulses. Judging is a continuation, along lines of expediency, of the original process by which the ego took things into itself or expelled them from itself, according to the pleasure principle. The polarity of judgment appears to correspond to the opposition of the two groups of drives which we have

> supposed to exist. Affirmation—as a substitute for uniting—belongs to Eros; negation—the successor to expulsion—belongs to the destructive drive. The general wish to negate, the negativism which is displayed by some psychotics, is probably to be regarded as a sign of a defusion of the drives that has taken place through a withdrawal of the libidinal components. But the performance of the function of judgment is not made possible until the creation of the symbol of negation has endowed thinking with a first measure of freedom from the consequences of repression and, with it, from the compulsion of the pleasure principle. (SE 19: 238-239; translation modified)

We know from the description of the experience of satisfaction that judgment in language is preceded by the judgment of reality. Moreover, what Freud says here is that the former is a continuation of the latter. We can therefore say, without fear of erring, that negation is the continuation of the oral or anal expulsion of the hated object. It is in this sense that negation is a sort of sui generis sublimation, because Freud's definition of sublimation suggests that it is a rerouting of a sexual drive. However, in the case of negation, what is rerouted is the destructive drive (one of the forms taken by the death drive, as we know). In short, negation's relation to the death drive involves a movement or passage from destructive action to sublimation in language, by way of the symbol of negation.

When it comes to the construction of ever more complex forms of social organization, then—that is, when it comes to the fundamental project of Eros—negation carves out a path for the sublimation of the death drive. Sublimation is thus not a mechanism that belongs only to the sexual drives. If negation is, we might say, a sophisticated form of the primary impulses to expel what displeases us, the result of this transaction turns out to be erotic, to be of the order of Eros. In this case, destruction passes from the "active" or "material" state to a state of "enunciation" or, again, mere "breath."

We have arrived at a point in our analysis of psychoanalytic theory that has taken us, with Freud, beyond Freud himself. As Ricoeur notes, within the parameters of what we could call the traditional interpretation of Freud (and those of Freud's own interpretation of himself, at his most Freudian), the death drive cannot be seen as related to creativity. When Freud says, in *Beyond the Pleasure Principle*, that the death drive never appears alone, that it is always accompanied by the life drive, that it is never simply present, that it only appears in the guise of Eros, I think that he is referring to a movement that runs counter to the movement of negation. Let us say that, in *Beyond the Pleasure Principle*, Freud is considering phenomena in psychic life in which the death drive and the life drive are confused, because they are interconnected in the same act of discharge. Sadomasochistic sexual relations are perhaps paradigmatic of these psychic phenomena. But in negation the destructive drive has a purely erotic aim and is expressed (discharged) in language rather than in action. Freud writes in "Negation," again:

> Judging is a continuation, along lines of expediency, of the original process by which the ego took things into itself or expelled them from itself, according to the pleasure principle. The polarity of judgment appears to correspond to the opposition of the two groups of drives which we have supposed to exist. Affirmation—as a substitute for uniting—belongs to Eros; negation—the successor to expulsion—belongs to the destructive drive. (SE 19: 239; translation modified)

As Ricoeur notes, it should not surprise us that negation displaces the death drive; it should surprise us instead that it fulfills a completely erotic function. And negation in judgment is not the only erotic substitute for the death drive. Both Ricoeur and Kristeva suggest that we should see the sublimation of the death drive in play and in aesthetic creation, defined as a "work of the negative": "The death drive is not closed in upon destructiveness, which is, we said, its clamor; perhaps it opens out onto other aspects of the 'work of the negative,' which remain 'silent,' like itself" (*Freud and Philosophy* 318).

In short, the fundamental point here is that the death drive can be absorbed into erotic functions, and that the latter all involve, first, semiotic functions (judgment in language, play, and aesthetic creation); and, second, a movement out into the world, an effort to communicate with and not to break the world or annihilate it. I am not denying language's capacity to harm and cause offense, or that discourse can also be an apparatus of power and therefore subjection and domination. But the difference is economic and not essential. The space that language opens in its address to the other tends to be broader than the space of physical violence. That is, any act of communication, however violent it may be, leaves open the possibility of response, leaves the subject alive—if only engulfed in living flame, if the speech act has been devastating. Such devastation still allows for the possibility that another might come to the rescue. It is true that the performative power of language, its force, taken to its logical extreme, can be annihilating. But although there is a space in which the force of language and physical violence overlap, there is another space in which acts of enunciation and acts of violence are differentiated, and it is this latter space that I am working to make visible.

Let us think, then, of another path for sublimation: play.

Although in *Beyond the Pleasure Principle* Freud relates his grandson's *fort-da* game[17] to the anxiety dreams caused by traumatic neuroses, there is a fundamental difference: The game is not driven by repetition compulsion. In anxiety dreams, according to Freud, the repetition of a trauma does not lead to the renunciation of a position of domination; anxiety arises as a preventative signal that prepares the subject for the traumatic blow to come. By contrast, the experience of the *fort-da* game is pleasurable and not anxious-making, precisely because the experience of the game involves a renunciation. In Freud's description, both the anxiety dream and the *fort-da* game stage the desire to play an active role (or what we could call the role of the agent). In the game Freud's grandson restaged his own abandonment by his mother. (Freud takes the reel that the boy throws to represent his mother. Throwing this reel "away" lets the boy disregard his mother rather than being disregarded by her, as he is in real life.) In anxiety dreams, meanwhile, anxiety functions as a signal that the subject is awaiting the traumatic event rather than being taken by surprise, as in the war. In play, the turning of a passive position into an active one follows from a sort of acceptance or renunciation that involves a different affective position than the one in anxiety dreams. Play creates the space in which active behavior can unfold erotically. In other words, the difference between dreaming and play would seem to be that whereas dreaming points to a lack or refusal of submission, this is the very operation that gives rise to playing.

According to Ricoeur, the work of art is also a sort of *fort-da* game that makes the object of fantasy disappear so that a cultural object can appear in its place:

> In Paragraph 6 [of "The Two Principles of Mental Functioning," Freud] says that art brings about a rec-

> onciliation between the two principles in a peculiar way: the artist, like the neurotic, is a man who turns away from reality because he cannot come to terms with the renunciation of instinctual satisfaction that reality demands, and who transposes his erotic and ambitious desires to the plane of fantasy and play. By means of his special gifts, however, he finds a way back to reality from this world of fantasy; he creates a new reality, the work of art, in which he himself becomes the hero, the king, the creator he desired to be, without having to follow the roundabout path of making real alterations in the external world. In this new reality other men feel at home because they "feel the same dissatisfaction as he does with the renunciation demanded by reality, and because that satisfaction, which results from the replacement of the pleasure principle by the reality principle, is itself part of reality." (*Freud and Philosophy* 333–334)

The problem that Ricoeur addresses just before this explication relates to a question that is fundamental to any effort to think of the sublimation not only of the sexual drives, but of the death drive as well: "Thus does not the death drive have as its normal, nonpathological expression the disappearing-reappearing in which the elevation of fantasy to symbol consists?" (*Freud and Philosophy* 314; translation modified). As I noted earlier, it is in this sense that Kristeva argues that language has a perverse structure in that it treats the word as a thing. We could say that in the realms of language, play, and art, fantasy and desire are transfigured, taking the form of words, ludic scenes, or cultural objects. What these three psychic operations share, then, is a perverse inversion: The original object of discharge has been exchanged in each case for an "as if," for an object treated "as if it were the original." This represents an incalculable gain in cultural terms, because it demonstrates that the psyche is or has a capacity for plasticity, that desire can be satisfied by all kinds of objects. To be clear, in strictly psychoanalytic terms, perversity refers not only to pathological conditions; it can also, as in the cases we are analyzing, shed light on the psyche's capacity to "metaphorize." Desire can thus be discharged on a culturally accepted object, ideally in a culture that, as Marcuse would say, is not excessively restricting, a culture in which the substitute object would facilitate sublimation rather than repression. This is (we can hope) the utopian promise of civilization (or the promise that has remained utopian until now). Recall that the pervert's sexual fetish that Freud takes to be exemplary is an object treated "as if" it were the lost object (paradigmatically, the penis "missing" from the female body). In the case of cultural objects, the subject treats them "as if" they were primary objects. Art, play, and the word therefore offer possibilities for happy discharge in the realm of the imaginary (which does not mean the realm of the unreal, the nonexistent, or the unrealizable). I am referring not only to the discharge of sexual drives, but also to the discharge of the drives to destruction and death. The forms of expression that we consider "cultural"—because, on the one hand, they can coexist with the social and legal spheres, and, on the other, they stand opposed to narcissistic forms and efforts to annihilate the other—are the privileges of speech. They let us recover in language, defined as a system of communication, the dynamics of sublimation, which constitute and are continually operative within language itself. As Kristeva notes, there is no language without creativity, because there is no language without sublimation.

If we follow Freud closely, we can see that negation is not a representative of the death drive, but rather a substitute for it. Already in *Beyond the Pleasure Principle*, we could see this relation between the two principles, the pleasure principle and the reality principle. In *Beyond*, the reality principle does not work against or negate the pleasure principle; on the contrary, the latter remains operative and continues to seek fulfillment. But the psyche cannot tolerate immediate discharge. The reality principle represents, as Derrida rightly emphasizes in his reading of *Beyond the Pleasure Principle*, the possibility of a detour, a deviation but not a renunciation of pleasure. Negation is, in this same sense, a detour or rerouting of the destructive drive, not a renunciation of it. Playing and art follow this same path. When Freud says that the study of judgment is the royal road to an understanding of negation and thinks of the latter as a path taken by the death drive, he is referring to the realm of language. There is thus a basis in Freud for the effort to connect the psyche to language defined as a semiotic function, since negation is implicated in language at every turn. Negation speaks through the patient who says, "No, she's not my mother," and the psychoanalyst knows that she is the patient's mother but displaced by a representation, that is, symbolized by another object that allows for fantasy, for dreaming, or for acting "as if the real were not." In the same way, art and play are also the irruptions of a negativity that cannot be reduced to destructiveness. In the symbolic, the death drive reveals its capacity not for pure destruction, but rather, on the contrary, for enjoyable creation, because it manages—again, in the imaginary—to overcome absence, passivity, loss, and the mediated satisfaction of desire in general.

To be sure, then, through negation, the psychic apparatus takes distance from the tendency to discharge tension. But we cannot therefore say that this tendency has been annulled, because the blockage of affect shows that the pleasure principle still operates. When the infant decides not to remain fixated on the subjective image of the object of satisfaction and turns instead toward the external world, it renounces one death, a short-circuiting of life, opting instead for the deferred or postponed death that is life itself.

This turning toward the world corresponds, then, to the renunciation of primary narcissism. In this moment, the organism decides not to die then and there, freely. It decides instead to subject itself to the laws of the Other in order to stay alive. But here we should emphasize that although this decision is archaic and precarious as well, it does guarantee that a crucial ontological deviation will take place. This is the "instant" when the organism has a choice between letting itself die and looking outward. Obviously this is not an intellectual decision. Following Freud's speculative gesture in *Beyond the Pleasure Principle*, we can venture to say that the decision has been made by life itself. What I mean is that negation shows us another power of Eros. In addition to being a way of sublimating the death drive, negation is an intellectual operation that opens onto two ways of affirming life. These two ways lead in opposite directions. First, when the subject says, "No, that woman I desire is not my mother," we sense its submission to the Law, a submission that it has accepted in order to stay alive in the eyes of, or under the threat of coercion by, institutional powers. In other words, in this statement, the speaking subject turns back on itself in order to negate its desire to transgress social prohibitions. Second, however, Freud manages to show that negation is also what gives rise to the differentiation between inside and outside, between the pleasure-ego (a primitive version of the ego) and the other. The recognition of this difference clearly implies a decision to turn toward the world, to be inscribed or to inscribe oneself into the social fabric, that is, to enter the realm of Eros.

Let us consider in a bit more depth the negativity that resides beyond destruction and that opens onto erotic possibility. In his book on Freud, Ricoeur poses more than one question about Freud's understanding of pleasure and its close connection to the negative in *Beyond the Pleasure Principle*. The first problem in Freud's text that Ricoeur points to is the notion that pleasure is a merely quantitative problem. Freud defines pleasure as a discharge of tension and unpleasure as an increase in tension. It is this formulation that immediately relates pleasure to the death drive, since discharge seeks to reach a zero degree of tension, that is, to arrive at the point of death. Freud had already "resolved" this problem by suggesting that the life drive brought about a modification in the pleasure principle, converting it into a principle of constancy. For Ricoeur, the principle of constancy is an *erotic* modification of the pleasure principle, so that pleasure can only be on the side of life. But the problem then becomes how to account for cruelty, given that pleasure can be taken in causing pain or even in bringing about another's death. Perhaps Ricoeur is right as long as we are thinking of the search for pleasure as only propelled by the life drive, but this does not mean that the modification of the pleasure principle affects *all* of it any more than it turns it into a search for Nirvana (which would associate it with the death drive). I am referring to the fact that for Freud the psyche does not develop according to a linear and progressive temporality. In other words, the interactions between different psychic mechanisms and even the stages of psychosexual development itself are never neutralized; instead they remain active. So the fundamental problem with experiences of pleasure caused by doing harm is not resolved by the intervention of Eros or the erotic modification of the pleasure principle, unless we think of this modification as ongoing, continuous, rather than once and done.

One of the most important characteristics of Eros is that it tends toward the other, that is, toward what alters it. In this way, Eros creates tension. If we follow Ricoeur's reformulation of *Beyond the Pleasure Principle*, then pleasure cannot be separated from love or, for that reason, from the creation of tensions. As Ricoeur rightly indicates, Freud had already said something about this when treating the economic problem of masochism. Considering sadism and masochism, Freud realizes that there are pleasures that can be experienced as unpleasure, and vice versa. He then concludes that pleasure must have something to do with time, periodicity, or the rhythm of discharge. Thus pleasure is not merely a quantitative matter, because quality, for Freud, already in the *Project for a Scientific Psychology*, is precisely a matter of rhythm, a rhythm of excitation (of ω neurons). In "The Economic Problem of Masochism," Freud argues that the pleasure principle is not a Nirvana principle, because the latter tends toward zero and therefore belongs to the death drive. By contrast, the pleasure principle, understood as a principle of constancy, entails the maintenance of a reserve of energy. That is, this principle keeps tension in reserve and therefore involves Eros.

On the other hand, the key distinction between instincts and drives is that the latter lead toward the other and are, according to Ricoeur, essentially erotic. Although this claim might seem to contradict Freud's understanding of the drive, if we pay attention to the economy of the erotic and destructive drives—the economy that Freud describes in "The Economic Problem of Masochism," another text that revises *Beyond the Pleasure Principle*—we can see that some forms of pain can cause pleasure, and some forms of pleasure can cause pain. That is, the erotic is always in play. To be sure, we could say the same thing about the death drive. But although Freud argues that all drives are conservative, for

Ricoeur, we must recognize that they are not all conservative to the same degree:

> [I]f the pleasure principle means nothing more than the principle of constancy, must it not be said that only Eros is beyond the pleasure principle? Eros is the great exception to the principle of constancy. I am well aware that Freud writes that all the instincts are conservative to a higher degree in that they are peculiarly resistant to external influences, and, in another sense, that they preserve life itself for a comparatively long period. Further, the hypothesis of a "sexuality of cells" allows one to interpret self-preservation and even narcissism as an "erotic" sacrifice of each cell for the good of the whole body, hence as a manifestation of Eros. Finally and above all, if Eros is "the preserver of all things," it is because it "unites all things." But this enterprise runs counter to the death drive. "Union with the living substance of a different individual increases those tensions, introducing what may be described as fresh 'vital differences' which must be lived off." Thus we have the sketch of an answer: that which escapes the principle of constancy is Eros itself, the disturber of sleep, the "breaker of peace." However, doesn't this proposition destroy the hypothesis that lies at the origin of psychoanalysis, namely that the psychical apparatus is regulated quasi-automatically by the principle of constancy? (*Freud and Philosophy* 320)

Indeed, it does. Eros conserves but also complicates; that is, it also moves away from Thanatos, which tends toward the preservation of what we could call a radically atomic identity. This other force that Freud calls the "exigency of life" or that, following Darwin, we could call the instinct for survival also operates in a quasi-automatic way, turning toward the other and encouraging the construction of complex organizations that create tension.

Humor and the Supremacy of the Ego

Before concluding these reflections, I would like to consider another detour and another way of sublimating destructiveness, one that very few readers of Freud have attended to: humor. In his book on jokes, Freud offers an economic explanation of humor, defined as a yield in pleasure that "arises from *an economy in the expenditure of affect*" (SE 8: 229; emphasis in original). When, hearing an anecdote, our expectations are disappointed, and the feeling that might "naturally" be associated with the anecdote can be overcome and even turned into its opposite, the psyche takes pleasure in this flight.

For Ricoeur, the key to the sublimating transaction involved in humor is fundamentally that it saves narcissism from catastrophe. This is, Ricoeur adds, a characteristic that can be identified in all intellectual activities that involve sublimation. Where, Ricoeur wonders, does humor derive its capacity for withdrawal and flight? In Freud's analysis in his 1927 text titled "Humour," he explains that the yield in pleasure in humor is afforded by the superego. As the psychic agency that is formed by the incorporation of parental law and of Law in general, the superego is a kind of psychic police force, a punishing figure, and, in Nietzschean terms, the place where bad conscience has installed itself. As we know, humor only arises in situations of devastation, in which the ego has been diminished and humiliated. The intellect's ability to bypass the superego's urgent demands is owing to the superego's willingness to relax for a moment, putting the ego in charge of the imperatives and demands of punitive psychic agencies or political and social institutions. So, Freud explains, "in bringing about the humorous attitude, the superego is actually repudiating reality and serving an illusion" (SE 21: 166). The ego creates its own world and its own rules, as in child's play or the other world of aesthetic creation.

Humor is a sublimating effort made by the psyche. Like all psychic procedures that manage to reroute or even bypass the repressive demands of punitive psychic agencies, humor follows the regressive path to the discharge of the drive:

> These last two features — the rejection of the claims of reality and the putting through of the pleasure principle — bring humour near to the regressive or reactionary processes which engage our attention so extensively in psychopathology. Its fending off of the possibility of suffering places it among the great series of methods which the human mind has constructed in order to evade the compulsion to suffer — a series which begins with neurosis and culminates in madness and which includes intoxication, self-absorption and ecstasy. (SE 21: 163)

Here we see once again that for Freud the difference between the normal and the pathological is merely one of degree, not one of kind. Although humor shares the same mechanisms as certain pathological processes, we should not lose sight of the fact that what both neurosis and psychosis seek to escape are the urgent demands of the world, incorporated into psychic organization. Here what sets humor apart is that it does not involve the loss either of the reality principle or of any ethical compass; it simply evades the latter for a few moments, where importantly this happens in the realm of the imaginary. It is, as Freud says, "liberating and elevating," for a moment, because it places the ego above the superego, that is, it makes the world appear as a children's game, the pastime of a sovereign subject that looks at the world from a place outside the law. The ego experiences "grandeur" in this moment and disparages laws, which are "for sheep."

The superego offers the ego a "yield of pleasure" by stepping away and laughing at reality. But Freud concludes that this capacity to take distance from the world of laws through humor is still somehow redolent of parental authority, and perhaps for this reason it is felt to be a safe realm, or a matter of what we could call an authorized rebellion: "It is also true that, in bringing about the humorous attitude, the superego is actually repudiating reality and serving an illusion . . . And finally, if the super-ego tries, by means of humour, to console the ego and protect it from suffering, this does not contradict its origin in the parental agency" (SE 21: 166).

Erotic battles must therefore be fiercely and unwaveringly fought:

> If the meaning of culture is a struggle of the human species for existence, if love is to be the stronger of the two [that is, of Eros and Thanatos], what is the meaning of the acceptance of death in relation to the enterprise of Eros? Does not the acceptance of death have to overcome a final counterfeit which would be precisely the death drive, the wish to die *against which* Eros is aimed? . . .
>
> Freud's philosophical temperament consists perhaps in this delicate equilibrium — or subtle conflict? — between lucidity free of illusion and the love of life. (*Freud and Philosophy* 336–337; translation modified)

The only thing that can be affirmed and even demanded of a battalion of pacifists is that those who take part in it should be intelligent enough to maintain their balance when walking this tightrope, where the secret is that in order to do so, one cannot stop moving. One can take a step back or even several, but only in order to regain balance and then move forward again, though not "forward" in a progressive sense, since the tightrope dos not lead to any door or destination. It is not even a straight line, in fact, but has the shape of an abyssal eternal return. But where does it return to? To a point that makes it possible to see the interminable need to keep going, because the cost of stopping on the tightrope would be an imminent fall. In other words, the forces of death, of Thanatos, can only be resisted by resisting, that is, in a gerundive, processual way. Thus erotic action, which works to create sublimating paths for the death drive, is an interminable task, and for Freud it shares this feature with psychoanalysis, education, and politics. We could say that these tasks are impossible, but this does not mean that they cease to be tasks; that is, an impossible task is still a task, still essentially something that must be done, a process that is never completed. Its time is gerundive, not the time of renunciation. These tasks are everlasting, because what the economy of human passions shows is that the death drive is insuperable. Still, at the same time, we have been able to glimpse the possibility of rerouting and displacing it or, in a psychoanalytic vocabulary, of delaying it, always radically postponing it, saving it for later. The erotic battalion cannot stop, cannot pause for breath. It fights in a duel that is not to the death, but that is ongoing, until death . . .

Let us recall the concluding warnings in Freud's texts on the problem of violence. From *Beyond the Pleasure Principle*: "What we cannot reach flying, we must reach limping . . . /The Book tells us it is no sin to limp" (SE 18: 64). And the last lines of Freud's letter to Einstein, "Why War?": "[W]hatever fosters the growth of civilization works at the same time against war" (SE 22: 215). As we have already seen, culture is a double-edged sword in that it gives rise to psychic pain and at the same time is our only path toward erotic complexity. We will need to devise strategies for resisting cultural or civilizational forms that seek out the simple, the homogenous, or the annihilation, exclusion, or marginalization of difference. We must instead promote those forms that encourage the construction of a plural, diverse, and tense public sphere.

Postscript

Toward a Community of Duelists

In *The Psychic Life of Power*, Judith Butler defines the subject as a site in which the paradox of subjection and agency is played out. This definition deconstructs the modern subject, because it no longer refers to an essence or ultimate foundation for the truth, logos, or reason. For Butler, the subject is instead a site in which a play of forces unfolds, where not all of these forces can be apprehended by the ego or "I." In other words, the subject is also the non-ego; it is an agency that has been subjected by the Law of the other, of others. Butler's theory of subjectivity is complex, and I will not treat it thoroughly here, but I would like to underscore the fact that the subject or, in Freudian terms, the psyche is a space of both vulnerability and resistance. Derrida gives the name *writing* to the phenomenon, or rather the economy, that best describes this space. I call this economy *alterability* not because writing is not already an economy of resistance, violence, and vulnerability for Derrida; rather, I want to emphasize the *alter-*, the alterity or otherness in alteration, as well as the resistance to alteration offered by the One or one. Vulnerability—and at the same time violence—is at the heart of the emergence of subjectivity. Moreover, for Derrida, Butler, and Freud—or rather, for Derrida and Butler, who follow Freud—life itself would be the difference between vulnerability and violence, where difference would be the result or remainder in this economy. The force of the other that is kept in reserve is, for example, the force of violence against the other, but also the force of violence against the self, because the one emerges precisely through resistance to the other, so that there cannot be one without the other.

But beyond a theory of subjectivity, what I would like to offer is a set of reflections on violence, vulnerability, and the resistance necessary to oppose annihilating levels of aggression. As Butler writes, "[S]peculations on the formation of the subject are crucial to understanding the basis of non-violent responses to injury and, perhaps most important, to a theory of collective responsibility" (*Precarious Life* 44). I believe that the key for thinking this whole dimension of life and of biopolitics in particular is thinking these three forces together: violence, vulnerability, and resistance. And of course one cannot be thought of without the others. Like psychic memory, the phenomenon of life in general can be explained by this economy. The psyche is an apparatus that originates in the struggle between two contradictory tendencies: the urgency of life and the drive to return to an inorganic state. For Freud, the psyche as machine is set in motion at the moment when, in the psychoanalytic myth, the first stimulus, which is always experienced as unpleasure, intrudes. In this instant, mechanisms for avoiding stimuli are activated, but at the same time this first stimulus has already made a mark. This trace is the result of the difference between the force of the organism's resistance (a sort of natural or a priori barrier against alteration from without) and the force of stimulation from the world. The inscription of the psyche thus leaves a sort of path that will mediate the discharge of tension; that is, this inscription makes the road to relief longer. The mark is a mnemic trace or archive that will delay death without overcoming it.

In sociopolitical terms, that is, in collective terms, the problem is how to resist violence and attend to vulnerability. And vulnerability is not a weakness to be overcome, but an opening to the other and to alteration. Vulnerability is also erotic, as Freud explains so well in his myth about the origin of life, where alteration sets life itself in motion. In *Beyond the Pleasure Principle*, Freud recounts that in the beginning all matter was inanimate until one vesicle was altered by another, and a mechanism in the former was activated such that it sought to counter this alteration (SE 18: 26). This expenditure of energy is nothing other than life itself. Though directed toward the recovery of an inanimate state, this is a path whose deviations can be erotic.

It is this ambivalent possibility that politics should take advantage of and cultivate. I am not referring only to state politics or institutional politics, but also to things more like care or what Foucault calls "virtue." In Butler's words:

> This becomes the signature mark of "the critical attitude" and its particular virtue. For Foucault, the question itself inaugurates both a moral and political attitude, "the art of not being governed or, better, the art of not being governed like that and at that cost." Whatever virtue Foucault here circumscribes for us will have to do with objecting to that imposition of power, to its costs, to the way in which it is administered, to those who do that administering. One might be tempted to think that Foucault is simply describing resistance, but here it seems that "virtue" has

> taken the place of that term, or becomes the means by which it is redescribed. ("What Is Critique?" n. p.)

On the other hand, for Butler, melancholia is a condition that shows us one of the horizons of the social, which is constituted by foreclosures.[1] Forbidden desires remain socially unrecognized, expelled from official records; having these desires leads to rejection, and this begins a melancholic circuit for some desiring subjects. In sociopolitical terms, the implications are enormous, because what melancholia shows us is that it is the social, moral, and political order that sets melancholic circuits in motion and keeps them going, because not all desiring subjects and not all bodies have a place in the world constituted by law.

Butler is right when she notes that melancholic circuits can be shot through with signifiers that have not been registered within the social fabric. Homosexual desire is the paradigmatic example at the center of Butler's analysis in *The Psychic Life of Power*, where it is defined as a foreclosed desire and turns out to offer a heuristic for understanding the melancholic circuits that are formed when desires are ignored or denied.

The collective realm, the public sphere, or the social structure does not necessarily need to be founded or administered on the basis of exclusions, marginalizations, or even annihilations and therefore also foreclosures or denials of forms of life or of subject positions. This is because nonviolent resistance to aggression is possible, meaningful, and indeed imperative. According to Hannah Arendt, Western ethics are based on the Socratic claim that it is better to suffer an injustice than to commit one (Plato, *Gorgias* 482d, e), and our whole legislative and juridical system has been designed with this in mind. But beyond the altruistic reasons we could find for following this ethical path, there are also other, selfish reasons to do so. If the one cannot be without the other, then it is alteration and the desire to avoid or counter it that set us all in motion. Membranes understood as limits between the one and the other are permeable, and in ethical and political terms they must be permeable for selfish as well as altruistic reasons. Although at the "end" of history, every one will disappear, erasure is not necessarily radical or the effect of annihilation. It can be the result of a history of alterations.

I noted earlier that, according to Freud's myth recounting the origin of the psyche and Derrida's account of the economy of writing, the survival of every singularity depends on its interaction or exchange with other organisms, that the world is a very complex ecosystem. But it is also true that every instant of interaction implies a transformation in which something is gained and at the same time something is lost, disappears, and dies. Although life is a history of alterations, it is at the same time a history of deaths that are not essentially "forced disappearances," but rather moments of metamorphosis.

We need to think of nonviolent ways to live together, not in a romantic and naïve sense, but rather as "duelists" [*duelistas*], as mourners in combat.[2] The public sphere should be a space for battalions or fencers who wield discourse, the word, or "the talking cure," in the beautiful formulation of Anna O., Freud and Breuer's patient, who used this phrase to refer to psychoanalytic treatment. Ontological and political difference should also be understood as sustaining the desire to affirm oneself in the other, in the public sphere, where this is not only a natural phenomenon or one inherent in life, but rather an effort that is ethically desirable and that should be promoted in the political realm.

I think of battalions of duelists because, in Spanish, *duelo* is erotic in both of its senses, defined both as mourning and as dueling. In both its everyday and its psychoanalytic senses, mourning [*duelo*], understood as the pain that follows a loss, implies that life is affirmed in the end. It is a period in which those left behind, those of us who are still alive, withdraw from the world and participate in a series of rituals to commemorate the loved, lost object. It is a time and a state in which the world as a whole seems to have lost if not all meaning, as in melancholia, then at least something very special. A *duelo* is also a duel or form of battle, one that need not lead to death but observes rules of engagement, and implies that the tension between the two forces is sustained. Although there is a winner, this victory does not compromise the other's life. If this struggle remains within the discursive realm, it will produce a democratic public sphere. The mourning "duelist" [*duelista*] thus turns out to be a figure for the democratic citizen whose political practice is erotic, because it is aggressive but not annihilating

As Freud indicates in "Mourning and Melancholia," "although mourning involves grave departures from the normal attitude to life, it never occurs to us to regard it as a pathological condition and to refer it to medical treatment. We rely on its being overcome after a certain lapse of time, and we look upon any interference with it as useless or even harmful" (SE 14: 243–244). A bit further on, he notes that we do not know why, after a time, life goes on, so to speak; in each case the duration of mourning is incalculable and singular. This remains an enigma. It is at this point that it becomes clear that mourning is a work of thought, and that the time of mourning is spent on transactions in which the libido invested in the lost object is finally withdrawn and displaced onto another object. Clearly, the very radical distinction that Freud makes at this point between two psychic phenomena, mourning and melancholia, would need to be qualified and amended. For example, it is important to point out that in ethical and political terms, as Derrida reminds us, it is not desirable that mourning should come to an end. History is also a history of deaths, whether unjust or otherwise, and it should be recognized as such. A quantity of libido must remain fixed on or invested in the object so that something of mourning remains, unspent. In other words, a certain measure of melancholia should persist to preserve the memory of what was lost and the meaning of that absence. As Derrida says, each loss is the loss of a whole possible world.

For Freud, again, the difference between the normal and the pathological is a quantitative and not a qualitative one. Freud's text on mourning performs the same gesture as *The Interpretation of Dreams*, redeploying Freud's favorite strategy: explaining the normal by way of the pathological. On countless occasions, Freud takes this path, and with good reason, because the relation between psychic disturbance and psychic tranquility is an economic relation, not a matter of identities. But what we should not forget is that it is the rhythm of the quantity that makes quality. Here again, I am referring to time and specifically to periods. From the point of view of psychoanalytic theory, we should think of differences of degree, of quantitative differences, that lead to qualities but not to essential differences. Correcting the quantitative model introduced in *Beyond the Pleasure Principle*, Freud writes in "The Economic Problem of Masochism":

> Pleasure and unpleasure, therefore, cannot be referred to an increase or decrease of a quantity (which we describe as 'tension due to stimulus'), although they obviously have a great deal to do with that factor. It appears that they depend, not on this quantitative factor, but on some characteristic of it which we can only describe as a qualitative one. If we were

> able to say what this qualitative characteristic is, we should be much further advanced in psychology. Perhaps it is the rhythm, the temporal sequence of changes, rises and falls in the quantity of stimulus. (SE 19:160)

In the earlier model of 1920 (in *Beyond the Pleasure Principle*), the experience of pleasure had to do exclusively with the reduction of stimuli, and that of pain with their augmentation. But Freud did not answer the question of *how* pleasure is felt. In his text on masochism, Freud addresses clinical cases in which the relation between pleasure and pain seems directly to contradict the definition of these terms offered in *Beyond the Pleasure Principle*:

> It seems that in the series of feelings of tension we have a direct sense of the increase and decrease of amounts of stimulus, and it cannot be doubted that there are pleasurable tensions and unpleasurable relaxations of tension. The state of sexual excitation is the most striking example of a pleasurable increase of stimulus of this sort, but it is certainly not the only one. (SE 19: 160)

In other words, we need to think of the time, or rather of the rhythm, of all stimulation or violence in order to account for the qualitative differences between these two experiences. Time is also crucial to the difference between mourning and melancholia. As I noted earlier, we should not think that the erotics of mourning—which makes it possible for us to love with the libido that has been freed for new and other objects—cannot have deathly consequences, or vice versa. Mourning and melancholia are psychic phenomena that not only live and work together; politically and ethically, we should also promote their coexistence so that it gives rise to a mourning that preserves something of melancholia, a melancholic remainder, after every loss. Because if we were fully to complete the work of mourning, then we would be left with no indignation or anger about the absence or disappearance of a possible world. We need indignation and anger in order to demand that the losses are not repeated. The difference, then, that lets us decide whether the outcome of a combined melancholic circuit and work of mourning is erotic or deathly would reside, first, in the quantity of libido left free for loving other objects. This difference, which would of course not be a matter of all or nothing, would be greater if mourning were to predominate, and lesser if melancholia were to preside over the process. But melancholic resistance to the reinvestment or displacement of the libido should not paralyze us. Instead it should lead to a mourning that would free libido for use in the battle against injustice. In Butler's words:

> If we forget that we are grieving, we become pure vessels of rage. If we forget to turn our rage into a demand for justice, we become pure destruction in the face of destruction. If we lose ourselves to sorrow, we lose the rage we need for the demand for justice and for the political future of freedom. ("Vulnerability and Resistance")

On the other hand, within the political sphere, mourning must preserve the memory of those lost and absent, because, as Derrida so clearly indicates, what disappears with each loss is a whole possible world. Thus despite the fact that we might well complain about what is lacking in the past—that is, something that should have been there—at the heart of the work of mourning is the renunciation of a future that was only possible with the lost object in it. What causes us to suffer so deeply are all the future possibilities that have been foreclosed by the loss. But mourning is precisely the psychic operation that at once brings about renunciation and opens new horizons.

Collective responsibility thus implies that we should be duelists, and this means occupying public space in order to struggle for justice. But this is not a battle to the death, because the task is precisely to sustain the political arena that allows for polemic, that is, for tension and opposition. In order to preserve the public sphere, we must keep the enemy alive, but the enemy must also care for us. The battle for justice is an eternal confrontation that, again, requires at least two different forces to protect the public sphere as such, that is, as shared and complex. Dueling defined as battle is the construction of history: the registration and naming of injustice, and the recognition not only of loss, but also of what was lost and its absence. Finally, the construction of such a history is the only practice that can prevent repetition, just as mourning and dueling are both practices that open onto the future as a horizon, as an unprecedented possibility.

Notes

Introduction

1. Parenthetical references with the abbreviation SE refer to the *Standard Edition* of Freud's works. SE is followed by the volume number and the page number. Sigmund Freud, *The Standard Edition of the Complete Psychological Works of Sigmund Freud*, 24 vols., translated by James Strachey et al. (London: Hogarth Press and the Institute for Psychoanalysis, 1953–1974).

2. By "hauntology," Derrida means an ontology besieged by ghosts.

3. In Spanish usage as well, the temporal and spatial meanings of *diferencia* have been forgotten. The Real Academia Española's *Diccionario de la lengua española* does recognize these meanings when it offers the following definition of *diferencia de fase* or "phase difference," a phrase used in physics and mathematics: "In two periodic processes, the *difference*, at a given moment, between the values of the two fractions of the period." But this is not what the word *diferencia* immediately evokes.

4. Undecidables are indeterminate concepts that show

us where the order of classification collapses. That is, they mark the limits of order and disturb the logic of oppositions. Undecidables do not have a determinate character or a character of their own; they involve a play of possibilities, a movement within and beyond oppositions. The supplement, for example, is undecidable because it is *at the same time* something that substitutes, that can take the place of, and something that is in excess, that adheres or is added to something else. It is important to clarify that, for Derrida, we cannot escape the undecidable, and deconstruction is not an effort to master undecidability.

5. But in addition, Freud errs when he interprets the time of consciousness as essentially linear and harmonious, because this linearity is only an illusion produced by the temporal implosion of mnemic writing.

6. I should clarify that by "writing" Derrida means a writing of traces, inscriptions, furrows, or tracks, and not phonetic writing. Phonetic writing would be committed to the metaphysics of presence to the extent that it lays claim to the ability to represent a (present) voice from the past, and to transmit the whole truth from one moment to another. In order to understand this idea better, it might help to think of the written text as a tissue or fabric or a floor in which holes have been drilled.

7. See Chapter 1, "The Economy of Alteration: Resistance and Violence."

8. In the interview "Eating Well, or the Calculation of the Subject," Derrida explains that in order to make decisions the subject engages in an ethical-political calculation about the possible consequences of its acts. Again, this is a phenomenological description that opens onto an ethical prescription. In other words, it is a fact that the subject calculates, acts, and makes decisions, but ethically we ought to take on these acts affirmatively: We act, and we have to act. This calculation is obviously and structurally shot through with an "incalculability"; it is what Derrida calls an "incalculable calculation." And it is incalculable because culture is a text, a hypertext that is constantly transformed by other subjects (where the subject is

understood in a broad sense, a sense including, for instance institutions, states, languages, and so forth). The impossibility of ethical-political calculation is, in temporal terms, twofold. Implosive time reveals that being is radically contingent; the movement of being in question, a movement between what "has been" in the past and makes itself felt in the present, on the one hand, and, on the other, the future at play in the now, or what "is without having been yet," makes the calculation impossible. Every decision or action transforms both history and the future, and this is a phenomenon that does not cease. Being is a constant becoming, and therefore Dasein can only act by making calculations that are structurally uncertain.

9. Derrida proposes the idea of an imperative to "go beyond the beyond" in "Psychoanalysis Searches the States of Its Soul: The Impossible Beyond of a Sovereign Cruelty." He refers, on the one hand, to Freud's *Beyond the Pleasure Principle*, where the death drive is presented as an insuperable tendency, and, on the other, to the unavoidable need to resist cruelty.

10. Eros is the force that tends toward the formation of organizations that are ever more complex; that is, it is a tendency toward union, toward addition, and not toward the destruction or elimination of synthesis: "Thus the libido of our sexual drives would coincide with the Eros of the poets and philosophers which holds all living things together" (SE 18: 50; translation modified).

11. Gender confirmation surgery—which was made possible in 1930 by advances in medicine—is a radical and paradigmatic example of how, from one moment to another, unprecedented forms of subjectivity can emerge that should be recognized juridically. In this case, an anatomical sex change suggests, as is clear from the positions taken by conservative groups, the need for a legal reform that would allow people to change the sex registered on their birth certificates. I do not mean that only trans people who undergo surgery should enjoy this right; my interest is in the illustrative nature of this example, since sexual identity is not a matter of birth or the genitals, and in much more general

terms this example points to the problem of the guest or the foreigner.

1. The Economy of Alteration: Resistance and Violence

1. *Translator's Note*: See also Bass's note on the translation of this term: "'Breaching' is the translation we have adopted for the German word *Bahnung*. *Bahnung* is derived from the German word *Bahn*, road, and literally means pathbreaking. . . . 'Breaching' is clumsy, but it is crucial to maintain the sense of the *force* that opens a pathway, and the *space* opened by this force; thus 'breaching' must be understood here as a shorthand for these meanings" (*Writing and Difference* 329n2).

2. The psychic apparatus would thus be an archive that attracts the world, through associations and as if with a magnetic force, as it is shaped by the writing of the world. Freud writes in his essay on repression: "The second stage of repression, *repression proper*, affects mental derivatives of the repressed representative, or such trains of thought as, originating elsewhere, have come into associative connection with it. On account of this association, these ideas experience the same fate as what was primally repressed. Repression proper, therefore, is actually an after-pressure [*Nachdrängen*]. Moreover, it is a mistake to emphasize only the repulsion which operates from the direction of the conscious upon what is to be repressed; quite as important is the attraction exercised by what was primally repressed upon everything with which it can establish a connection. Probably the trend towards repression would fail in its purpose if these two forces did not co-operate, if there were not something previously repressed ready to receive what is repelled by the conscious" (SE 14: 148).

3. The Greek language distinguishes between two kinds of life, *zoé* and *bios*. *Zoé* evokes infinite or unlimited life, whereas *bios* names singular and qualified life. *Bios* points to singular lives or the margins that separate some lives from others; it also refers to being in the world in one way or another (Kerényi 12–15).

2. The Economy of Sacrifice: Melancholic Elaborations

1. I mean "economy" in a double sense: this is both a monetary economy, to be sure, and above all an economy as it is defined in Freudian psychoanalysis, in which an organization is not a structure but rather the effect of a specular relation with other formations. (See Chapter 1 in this book, "The Economy of Alteration: Resistance and Violence.")

Every regulation is shaped by an economy. Regulation always implies a certain calculation, relying on particular laws. "Economy" should thus be understood in this text in its original sense, that is, as related to the Greek roots words *oïkos* and *nomos*, as the law of the dwelling, of the home, of domestic goods, and so forth. In totemic societies, on the one hand, the incest taboo and the prohibition of cannibalism were economic regulations in that they involved exogamous "exchanges" or "transactions" of women from distinct groups, and of meats that could be eaten. On the other hand, totemic laws regulated precisely this: the domestic, the most intimate sphere, the social nucleus and its primal desires.

2. But it is necessary to add that throughout *Totem and Taboo*, Freud assumes, first, that the guilt over parricidal desire is almost as strong as the guilt of having committed the crime; and, second, that the phylogenetic guilt over the committed crime corresponds to the ontogenetic guilt provoked by the desire. In *Moses and Monotheism*, Freud distinguishes between material truth and historical-experiential truth. The latter is a construction built not on the basis of a fact, but on the basis of an interpretation of a fact or even an idea whose effects are overwhelming. The myth of the totemic meal (or act, since Freud never decides between the two in *Totem and Taboo*), the reconstruction of the life of Moses in *Moses and Monotheism*, and the case of the "Wolf Man" are all paradigmatic examples of the force with which some fictions can guide the destiny both of the subject and of the history of a community. In all of these cases, Freud emphasizes that it is irrelevant whether an act was committed materially,

or in fact took place. It does not matter whether the primal horde in fact ate their father; it is irrelevant whether the Jews really killed Moses; the Wolf Man might have been witness to his parents' lovemaking, or he might not have been. The power of the virtual, of the intangible, is capable of causing the same psychic or historical effects as that of the actual. The mere desire to murder, the mere fantasy of playing a part in the Oedipal scene—these can produce the same traumatic effects as the acts themselves. Any civilization is founded on guilt over parricidal and incestuous desires. All Jewish culture revolves around what was at least an attempt to assassinate Moses. The madness of the Wolf Man is etiologically explicable if we refer to the fantasy and desire that involves bearing witness to the scene of his parents having sex. Although on some occasions we can distinguish between material and historical truth (and I would say this is only a matter of the "amount" of testimony, of the number and "nature" of witnesses, where their "nature" is defined by power relations), when it comes to effects and fantasized or fulfilled desires, the difference is immaterial.

3. For Freud, the paradigmatic figure for this mechanism is the fetishist, who denies the fact of feminine castration through the use of the fetish, even while he knows that the woman does not have a penis. See Freud, "Fetishism."

4. We should even cast doubt on the idea that the death penalty is a form of punishment, since a punishment is the payment of a "debt" in the public realm, a debt owed to a community, society, state, or nation whose repayment allows for both the reparation of damage and the subject's redemption. The death penalty closes off the latter possibility precisely.

5. By "unclonable," I do not mean technologically impossible to clone—since we know that it has been possible to clone a living organism for several decades now. I am referring instead to the unrepeatable, the singular, that is, to the impossibility of a "cloned" or pure or full repetition in spatiotemporal terms. Although we could say, using the terms in which Derrida thinks and writes, that singularity is iterability defined as "repetition

in difference," in this context my aim is to call attention to a "difference" that is significant in ethical-political terms.

6. Two questions following from this point call for clarification. First, the subject must deny this "passionate attachment," as Butler calls it, since the "I" is the site of self-consciousness and subjectivation and also the site where the inside is differentiated from the outside and from others. In this sense, the ego or "I," which Freud rightly defines as a site of identifications (where the subject identifies with others in its history), gains its autonomy (an autonomy that we know can only ever be partial) by denying its debts to others, its attachments, and its abiding dependencies.

7. Here it is helpful to recall Freud's text "Remembering, Repeating, and Working Through," which explains how action becomes a substitute for remembering and vice versa. As long as repression remains unresolved, the psyche must expend enormous amounts of energy in the form of resistance, whereas when repression is weakened, impulses are discharged in actions. By contrast, since the analysis of repression leads to remembering, Freud says, it takes the place of "acting out." In other words, the work of analysis enables the psyche to remember and impulses to remain within the realm of psychic imagining. I will examine this phenomenon in more detail in Chapter 3.

8. The sacrifice to which I am referring is not only a matter of the singular subject's desire to do something socially prohibited. I am referring instead to social sacrifices that communities make, sacrificing certain groups whose desires are condemned: gay people, psychotics, sex workers, poor people, *morenos* or brown people, *nacos* or "ghetto" people, and so forth. As Butler rightly notes in *The Psychic Life of Power*, the social or communal abandonment of these groups follows from their association with death, where death is defined not only biologically but also psychically in the sense that these groups are invisible to the state and the law. Rights thus should not be understood as limited to the constitutional realm; they must be taken to refer to a broader sense of visibility. To be sure, this must sometimes be translated

into law, but it is not only or always a matter of law, because there are ethical obligations that remain outside of this domain and that the state should still recognize.

9. I will return later to the problem of melancholia defined in specifically sociopolitical terms, in order to offer speculations on some possible erotic paths for the discharge of the drive.

10. Although Freud includes sublimation among the destinations of the drive, I think it can be thought of as a mechanism of defense, first because if the psyche is an apparatus, it is mechanical and therefore all psychic processes are mechanisms; and second because the destinations of the drives name the paths along which psychic forces are diverted and transformed so that they do not intrude on consciousness. We are thus dealing with psychic processes that protect consciousness from certain psychic stimuli that might cause discontent. Freud says in "Instincts and their Vicissitudes" that "we may also regard these vicissitudes as modes of *defence* against the drives" (SE 14: 127; translation modified).

11. See the Postscript to this book.

12. I am referring to the character in Herman Melville's story "Bartleby, the Scrivener."

3. Beyond the Limit of the Death Drive: Eros

1. I mean "ecology" not in the sense of the "green" ideology of environmental activism, but rather as a name for a strand of ontological thought in which the "one" is an effect of transversal relations with others. The one is in this sense the "echo" of the other. For a more in-depth discussion of this idea, see Félix Guattari, *The Three Ecologies*.

2. Here I am thinking of the formula that Derrida uses in his book *The Work of Mourning* (published in French as *Chaque fois unique, la fin du mond* and in Spanish as *Cada vez única, el fin del mundo*) to indicate that when death occurs, the irruption of absence that it causes changes the world, marking the end of the world each time it takes place. That is, the world that was

only possible because of the presence of the one who has now been lost—this world vanishes altogether. This reflection sheds light on the reason we must struggle against deaths imposed by other forces, forces that are not one's own or *appropriated* (in the Heideggerian sense of the term), because life is the only thing that is open to metamorphosis. By this I do not mean that action should never be guided by the aim of destroying violent or oppressive politics or practices. I mean instead that the political realm is a space where tension is sustained, and for this reason it must be possible for all contending parties to occupy public space.

3. In "The Economic Problem of Masochism," Freud explains the relationship between these two tendencies as a sort of mixing and unmixing of quantities of the same: "So far as the psychoanalytic field of ideas is concerned, we can only assume that a very extensive fusion and amalgamation, in varying proportions, of the two classes of drives takes place, so that we never have to deal with pure life drives or pure death drives but only with mixtures of them in different amounts. Corresponding to a fusion of drives of this kind, there may, as a result of certain influences, be a defusion of them" (SE 19: 164; translation modified).

4. Chapter IV in *Beyond the Pleasure Principle* opens this way: "What follows is speculation, often far-fetched speculation, which the reader will consider or dismiss according to his individual predilection. It is further an attempt to follow out an idea consistently, to see where it will lead" (SE 18: 24).

5. Derrida uses this phrase, life death, to name the paradoxical phenomenon in several of his texts. We should pay attention to each detail in the writing of this name, which brings together two Derridean gestures that do violence to language and its official use. First, "life" comes before "death," and I interpret this sequence as an indication of the emphasis that Derrida wanted to place on deconstruction defined as an affirmation of life, thus opposing the bad readings of those who saw deconstruction as a negative theology. Second, there is a space between these words,

without conjunction or disjunction; this makes it impossible to decide whether we are dealing with one noun or two. As Mónica Cragnolini said in a talk on Derrida that she gave on May 20, 2005, at the Universidad Nacional del Litoral, in Santa Fe, Argentina—a talk called "Adieu, Adieu, Remember Me: Derrida, la escritura y la muerte," this formulation brings together "two words that are united without union."

6. In Chapter 1, I offer a detailed analysis of psychic inscription, and I explain why both memory and the psyche are constituted by writing.

7. I explain this phenomenon in greater detail in Chapter 1.

8. For Derrida, space and time are not two distinct categories but rather one, because the appearance of being requires both at one and the same time, their coexistence. Derrida writes: "There is a *with* of time that makes possible the *with* of space, but which could not be produced as *with* without the possibility of space" (*Margins* 55). *Différance* is the neographism that refers to the ontological origin (or ~~origin~~) that indicates this co-appearance precisely.

9. The death drive is also an ontological limit that can be traced back to the origin of life in resistance to otherness.

10. See Jacques Derrida, "To Speculate—On Freud," in *The Post Card* 257–409, 359.

11. I say "philosophizing" here because, for Freud, the fundamental difference between psychoanalytic thinking and philosophical thinking was precisely that the latter reached its conclusions by way of speculation, whereas psychoanalysis had an empirical basis. On more than one occasion, Freud acknowledged that he had reached the same conclusions as some philosophers, but he maintained that his conclusions were of greater epistemological value since they were empirically grounded. If we were to be more faithful to Freud than he was to himself, then we would have to shelve his theory of the death drive, since it is deduced speculatively. In this way, Chapter IV of *Beyond the Pleasure Principle* would have to be set aside, regarded as not part of psychoanalytic theory, treated as a philosophical excursus.

12. This is Freud's conclusion in his *Project for a Scientific Psychology*, when he introduces ω neurons into his neurological fiction, because neither φ nor ψ neurons can explain the perception of quality. φ and ψ neurons are only capable of receiving or resisting quantities of stimulation, and Freud wonders how it is possible, given this fact, for us to perceive qualities. He concludes that a third kind of neuron is necessary, the ω neuron, which is capable precisely of perceiving the rhythm of stimulation. It is this, for Freud, that lends quality to the stimulation's force. On the other hand, twenty-five years later in "The Economic Problem of Masochism," confronting the problem that both masochism and sadism present for his theory of the supremacy of the pleasure principle, since both are forms of sexual conduct that do not involve a simple search for pleasure, but rather the discovery of pleasure in pain, Freud says: "Pleasure and unpleasure, therefore, cannot be referred to an increase or decrease of a quantity (which we describe as a 'tension due to stimulus'), although they obviously have a great deal to do with that factor. It appears that they depend, not on this quantitative factor, but on some characteristic of it, which we can only describe as a qualitative one. If we were able to say what this qualitative characteristic is, we should be much further advanced in psychology. Perhaps it is the *rhythm*, the temporal sequence of changes, rises and falls in quantity of stimulus. We do not know" (SE 19: 160; emphasis added).

13. In his text on sublimation, Hans W. Loewald argues that all of the destinations for the drive are in fact defenses against it. To the extent that their purpose is to reduce tension, they belong to the economy of the death drive. However, in sublimation, what takes place is a transformation of the drive, whose "original" goal is inhibited and whose object is displaced. At the same time, a process of cultural mediation redirects the search for pleasure (or to discharge the drive) toward human activities that are valorized and thought of as superior: art, religion, and science. It seems to me that, on the one hand, the erotics of sublimation result in a mediated form of discharge, where, as we saw in earlier chapters, this temporal delay or displacement is the work of the

life drive; on the other hand, these erotics mean that the activities that promote sublimation are themselves collective, that is, that they imply a tension and encounter with otherness. See Loewald, "Sublimation."

14. I write "re-presentation" here in keeping with Derrida's claim in "The Theater of Cruelty and the Closure of Representation" that every presentation is always a re-presentation: "The present offers itself as such, appears, presents itself, opens the stage of time or the time of the stage only by harboring its own intestine difference, and only in the interior fold of its original repetition, in representation. In dialectics" (*Writing and Difference* 248). Or: "The stage will no longer operate as the repetition of a *present*, will no longer *re*-present a present that would exist elsewhere and prior to it, a present whose plenitude would be older than it, absent from it, and rightfully capable of doing without it: the being-present-to-itself of the absolute Logos, the living present of God. Nor will the stage be a representation, if representation means the surface of a spectacle displayed for spectators. It will not even offer the presentation of a present, if present signifies that which is maintained *in front* of me. Cruel representation must permeate me. And nonrepresentation is, thus, original representation, if representation signifies, also, the unfolding of a volume, a multidimensional milieu, an experience which produces its own space" (*Writing and Difference* 237).

15. Here I treat the erotic and the conservative as opposed, knowing full well that the life drives work to conserve the living as such. Nevertheless, these drives do so by making organizations more complex, not by seeking a state of simple unity. I refer to "erotic sublimation" as if there were other kinds, and indeed it seems to me that there are, since there is no psychic phenomenon that is not fused with other phenomena. Although all sublimation is erotic, in that sublimation implies an affirmation of life, it also bears within itself the renunciation of the path toward an object. So according to Freud, Leonardo renounces active homosexual activity in favor of compulsive scientific research. It is in this sense that we might accuse

such sublimation of being conservative in that it does not challenge or defy the sociopolitical order and thus does not modify it or open new paths for the drive. Beyond the basic historical question of whether Leonardo acted on his homosexual desires, he could have died, and his choice of sublimation was erotic in this sense, even if it was also in some sense conservative and destructive or at least self-destructive. Of course, it is difficult to classify sublimation as either erotic or conservative, but this classification is relevant to the effort to create psychic space for a politics of nonviolence, a politics that would also alleviate suffering caused by self-inflicted damage and superegoic punishment.

16. See in this chapter the section titled "Humor and the Supremacy of the Ego," where I consider the place of humor in the organization of the psyche.

17. This is the name that Freud gives to the game that his grandson never tires of playing: he throws a wooden reel with a piece of string tied to it over the edge of a cot, only to make it return. He makes sounds resembling the word *fort* ("away" in German) when the reel disappears and *da* ("there" in German) when it returns. Freud's observation of this game was one of the phenomena that led him to doubt the supremacy of the pleasure principle in psychic life, since most of the time the boy only threw the reel away, and Freud thinks this object represents the boy's mother. Freud doubts that this way of taking distance from the mother represents a yield in pleasure for the boy, because, Freud tells us, the mother and the boy were very close and had a very good and affectionate relationship. Still, like all of the phenomena analyzed in Freud's text, the game is in keeping with the pleasure principle in that the yield in pleasure resides in the boy's ability to play an active rather than passive role (SE 18: 17).

Postscript: Toward a Community of Duelists

1. "Under social conditions that regulate identifications and the sense of viability to this degree, censorship operates implicitly and forcefully" (Butler, *Precarious Life* xx).

2. *Translator's Note*: In Spanish, the word *duelo* can mean both "duel" and "mourning." The author relies on this double sense of *duelo* throughout these pages, which also depend on the dual *duelista*, defined as both a duelist and a mourner, as a figure of both combat and collective grief.

Bibliography

Austin, J. L. *How to Do Things with Words*. Oxford: Oxford University Press, 1976.

Butler, Judith. *The Force of Nonviolence: An Ethico-Political Bind*. London: Verso, 2020.

———. *Precarious Life: The Powers of Mourning and Violence*. London: Verso, 2004.

———. *The Psychic Life of Power: Theories in Subjection*. Stanford, CA: Stanford University Press, 1997.

———. "Vulnerability and Resistance Revisited." Lecture presented at the National Autonomous University of Mexico, Mexico City, Mexico. March 23, 2015. webcast.unam.mx/?tribe_events=conferencia-vulnerabilidad-y-resistencia-revisitadas-imparte-la-dra-judith-butler.

———. "What Is Critique?: An Essay on Foucault's Virtue." *Transversal*, May 2001. http://eipcp.net/transversal/0806/butler/en.

Cragnolini, Mónica B. "Adieu. Adieu. Remember me. Derrida, la escritura y la muerte." Lecture presented at the conference "Jornadas Derrida," held at the Universidad Nacional del

Litoral, May 20, 2005. https://redaprenderycambiar.com.ar/derrida/co-mentarios/derrida_muerte.html.
——, "Derrida: Deconstrucción y pensar en las 'fisuras.'" Lecture presented at the conference "El pensamiento francés contemporáneo," held at the Alianza Francesa, Buenos Aires, Argentina. September 30, 1999.
——. "Una ontología asediada por fantasmas: El juego de la memoria y la espera en Derrida." *Escritos de filosofía* 41–42 (2002): 235–241.
Derrida, Jacques. *Archive Fever: A Freudian Impression.* Translated by Eric Prenowitz. Chicago: University of Chicago Press, 1996.
——. "Eating Well, or the Calculation of the Subject: An Interview with Jacques Derrida." Translated by Peter Connor and Avital Ronell. In *Who Comes After the Subject?* 255–287. Edited by Eduardo Cadava, Peter Connor, and Jean-Luc Nancy. New York: Routledge, 1991.
——. *The Gift of Death.* Translated by David Wills. Chicago: University of Chicago Press, 1996.
——. *Margins of Philosophy.* Translated by Alan Bass. Chicago: University of Chicago Press, 1985.
——. *The Politics of Friendship.* Translated by George Collins. London: Verso, 1997.
——. *The Post Card: From Socrates to Freud and Beyond.* Chicago: University of Chicago Press, 1987.
——. "Psychoanalysis Searches the States of Its Soul: The Impossible Beyond of a Sovereign Cruelty." In *Without Alibi*, edited and translated by Peggy Kamuf, 238–280. Stanford, CA: Stanford University Press, 2002.
——. *Specters of Marx: The State of Debt, the Work of Mourning, and the New International.* Translated by Peggy Kamuf. New York: Routledge, 1994.
——. *The Work of Mourning.* Edited by Pascale-Anne Brault and Michael Naas. Chicago: University of Chicago Press, 2001.
——. *Writing and Difference.* Translated by Alan Bass. Chicago: University of Chicago Press, 1978.

Eco, Umberto. A *Theory of Semiotics*. Bloomington: Indiana University Press, 1976.

Foucault, Michel. *Discipline and Punish: The Birth of the Prison*. Translated by Alan Sheridan. New York: Vintage, 1995.

Freud, Sigmund. *The Standard Edition of the Complete Psychological Works of Sigmund Freud*. 24 vols. Translated by James Strachey et al. London: Hogarth Press and the Institute for Psychoanalysis, 1953–1974.

Guattari, Félix. *The Three Ecologies*. Translated by Ian Pindar and Paul Sutton. 2000. London: Continuum, 2008.

Hanns, Luiz Alberto. *Diccionario de términos alemanes de Freud*. Buenos Aires: Lumen, 2001.

Heidegger, Martin. *Being and Time: A Translation of* Sein und Zeit. Translated by Joan Stambaugh. Albany: State University of New York Press, 1996.

———. "The Question concerning Technology." In *The Question concerning Technology and Other Essays*. Translated by William Lovitt. New York: Garland, 1977.

Hyppolite, Jean. "A Spoken Commentary on Freud's 'Verneinung.'" In Jacques Lacan, *Écrits: The First Complete Edition in English*, 746–754. Translated by Bruce Fink in collaboration with Héloïse Fink and Russell Grigg. New York: Norton, 2006.

Kant, Immanuel. *To Perpetual Peace: A Philosophical Sketch*. Translated by Ted Humphrey. Indianapolis: Hackett, 2003.

Kerényi, Karl. *Dionisios: Raíz de la vida indestructible*. Translated by Adan Kovacsics. Barcelona: Herder, 1998.

Kristeva, Julia. "The Impudence of Uttering: The Mother Tongue." Translated by Anne Marsella. www.kristeva.fr /impudence.html.

Loewald, H. W. "Sublimation: Inquiries into Theoretical Psychoanalysis." In *The Essential Loewald: Collected Papers and Monographs*. Hagerstown, MD: University Publishing Group, 2000.

Marcuse, Herbert. *Eros and Civilization: A Philosophical Inquiry into Freud*. 1955. Boston: Beacon Press, 1966.

Martínez Ruiz, Rosaura, "The Alterability of the Memory Trace." *Psychoanalytic Review* 98, no. 4 (2011): 531–555.
Melville, Herman. "Bartleby, the Scrivener: A Story of Wall Street." In *Billy Budd, Bartleby, and Other Stories*. New York: Penguin, 2016.
Plato. *Gorgias*. Translated by Donald J. Zeyl. Indianapolis: Hackett, 1987.
Ricoeur, Paul. *Freud and Philosophy: An Essay on Interpretation*. Translated by Denis Savage. New Haven: Yale University Press, 1970.

Rosaura Martínez Ruiz is Full Professor of Philosophy at the Universidad Nacional Autónoma de México. She is the author of two books in Spanish and is a member of the advisory board of the International Consortium of Critical Theory Programs.

Ramsey McGlazer is Assistant Professor of Critical Theory in the Department of Comparative Literature at the University of California, Berkeley. He is the author of *Old Schools: Modernism, Education, and the Critique of Progress*.

Judith Butler is Maxine Elliot Professor of Comparative Literature and in the Program in Critical Theory at the University of California, Berkeley. Their most recent book is *The Force of Nonviolence*.

www.ingramcontent.com/pod-product-compliance
Ingram Content Group UK Ltd.
Pitfield, Milton Keynes, MK11 3LW, UK
UKHW020831290926
15470UKWH00007B/1830

9 780823 298273